We're All Kin

We're All Kin

A CULTURAL STUDY
OF A
MOUNTAIN NEIGHBORHOOD

F. Carlene Bryant

THE UNIVERSITY OF TENNESSEE PRESS
KNOXVILLE

THIS BOOK IS THE WINNER OF THE FOURTH
James Mooney Award

*Clothbound editions of University of Tennessee Press books
are printed on paper designed for an effective
life of at least 300 years, and binding materials are
chosen for strength and durability.*

Library of Congress Cataloging in Publications Data

Bryant, F   Carlene, 1944-
  We're all kin.

  Bibliography: p.
  Includes index.
  1. Family—Tennessee—Case studies. 2. Tennessee—
Social life and customs. 3. Mountain life—Tennessee.
  4. Tennessee—Religious life. I. Title.
  HQ555.T3B78   976.8   81-473
  ISBN 0-87049-312-4   AACR1

To Harry Davitian
MY CLOSEST KINSMAN

CONTENTS

FIGURES

PREFACE

I first visited the neighborhood known as the top of the mountain very early one morning in October 1974. I went there to visit Seth Campbell, who had invited me to drop by around six o'clock to sample some of his homemade wine preliminary to a tour of the mountains. The wine occupied us longer than I had expected, and we did not get on the road until well after eight o'clock that morning. The day was nonetheless a very productive one: we visited two elementary schools, a health clinic housed in a trailer parked up a narrow hollow, a coal mine, and several general stores and private homes.

Seth Campbell, a retired coal miner, lives with his second wife and the two youngest of his twelve children in a small community perched on a narrow bench or ledge near the summit of one of the Cumberland Mountains in East Tennessee. His house, a modest four-room, wood frame structure, is located on a twisting dirt road about two miles south of the county highway, the only paved road passing through the mountains in these parts. Seth was about seventy-five years old when I met him in 1974 and had been retired from mining for some time. His retirement years have been far from idle,

however. In addition to farming his twenty-eight-acre property, he has been actively working for many years to improve
health care in the mountains and has recently helped to establish a free health clinic in an old mining community near his
home.

At the time I met Seth Campbell, I had just undertaken a
research project for the University of Tennessee's Appalachian
Resources Project to examine the social effects of surface mining in mountain neighborhoods. I began driving up to the
mountains frequently from my home in Oak Ridge, only
about forty-five minutes away, and revisited the people I had
met through Seth and through other acquaintances. They introduced me to their friends and neighbors, almost invariably
their near or distant kin, and I soon knew, at least in passing,
many people residing throughout the area.

For my research on surface mining I focused on portions
of only two neighborhoods, however, and I therefore came
to know best the people residing in these locales. These two
neighborhoods, called the top of the mountain and Isaac's
Creek, are about three miles from one another, the former
situated, as noted, close to a mountain summit and the latter
stretched out along a creek in a narrow valley at the western
foot of that mountain. Within a short time I was visiting these
neighborhoods almost daily: conducting a household census,
eliciting genealogies, chatting with residents about land, mining, families, and so forth, and mapping the homes, roads,
creeks, and strip pits of the area.

In the course of my work I participated in a variety of
neighborhood and area activities: quilting bees, church services, revivals, baby showers, and family reunions, for example. I often joined a small group of women in their almost
continuous winter quilting bee; throughout the season each
woman in strict rotation brought a patchwork spread, batting,
and lining to be stretched and worked on a frame occupying
most of the floor area of a spare bedroom in the home of one
of the women. One Sunday I went to the funeral of a former

area resident who was being buried back home; after the service the coffin was placed on a bed of a four-wheel drive pickup, which, followed by a number of similar trucks carrying family members and guests, forded two creeks and climbed a muddy and deeply rutted road to a small family cemetery located on the by then uninhabited top of a mountain. Another time I took a casserole to a covered dish dinner that the families living along a side road were hosting for the county road crew who had been blacktopping their road. And one day I tagged along with a man who was exploring for water with a forked stick; his search was successful, for later that day several neighborhood men found water when, following his advice, they dynamited a dry well and broke through to an underground stream. It was through informal participation in these kinds of events and activities as much as or more than through my direct questions and interviews that I came to know the people of the area.

On my early visits to the mountains I was sometimes accompanied by my mother-in-law, Sarah Davitian. She is an Armenian woman, born and raised in the Middle East, who has lived most of her life in New York City. For her, these visits to the mountains were steps into a radically different world; and her reactions and comments, particularly on the style of mountain religious services, were often intriguing, informed as they were by perspectives quite different from my own. To the people she met in the mountains, Sarah was the object of considerable polite interest, and despite some linguistic barriers, she and they came to like one another very much; her occasional visits no doubt greatly enhanced my own reputation.

In the spring of 1975 I completed my research on surface mining, but I continued to visit the mountains regularly. In May I moved up to the top of the mountain, where I resided for most of the summer with a family in Bradley Flats, one of four communities composing the neighborhood. Later, intrigued by several problems related to the nature and role of kinship, I decided to write my doctoral dissertation on the subject, and I returned to live with the same family in the summer of 1976. This book exploring the principles underlying the social organization of the top of the mountain, one of the two neighborhoods I initially worked in, is a revision of that dissertation.

"The top of the mountain" is the phrase actually used by area residents to refer to the neighborhood that is the subject of this book; it has no formal designation and to my knowledge is not noted on any map. However, to preserve anonymity all other local place names, including that of the county in which the top of the mountain is located, and all personal and family names, are fictitious.

Acknowledgments

Special thanks and acknowledgments are due to a number of people:

To the residents of the top of the mountain, who graciously welcomed me to their neighborhood and assisted me throughout my period of research there. I am especially grateful to the members of the household with whom I resided during my stays on the mountain, for they always made me feel at home, like part of the family.

To a former resident of the mountain who has been interested for many years in her late husband's family history. She generously shared the results of her extensive genealogical research with me and immeasurably facilitated my work.

To Robert Smith for agreeing that a Tennessee mountain neighborhood might be an interesting thesis topic and for his editorial suggestions; to Carole Greenhouse, Ruth Borker, Bernd Lambert, Danny Maltz, Allen Batteau, and Miles Richardson for their many bibliographic leads and their thoughtful suggestions and comments.

KEY TO HOUSEHOLDS
DEPICTED IN GENEALOGICAL FIGURES

1. Ernest and Susan Green
2. Bill and Pat Green
3. Luther and Mary Campbell
4. Seth and Joanna Campbell
5. Fred and Grace Bradley
6. Gladys Lewis (widow of Garrett Lewis)
7. Madge Johnson (ex-wife of Wilbur Johnson)
8. Fred and Carla Lewis
9. Wilbur, Jr. and Louise Johnson
10. Sam and Maude Hamilton
11. Jed and Susan Hamilton
12. Bobby and Liz Hamilton
13. Dave and Ann Riley
14. Martha and Bobby Mitchell Johnson
15. Ron and Tammy Morris
16. Greg and Lois Morris
17. Jed and Sally Jones
18. Barbara Johnson (widow of Bobby Johnson)
19. Lathrop and Debbie Stone
20. Dan and Rosie Dalton
21. Larry and Tula Bradley
22. Mabel Dalton (widow of Bratcher Dalton)
23. Eli and Alice Jones
24. Pete and Lucy Dalton
25. Houston and Frances Jones
26. Cal and Marj Jones
27. Sarah Bradley (widow of Riley Bradley)
28. Dave and Cleta Randolph
29. Nora and Luther Hamilton
30. Earl and Nellie Bradley
31. Lizzie and Bob Bradley
32. James and Carol White
33. Wayne and Connie Bradley
34. Vester and Barbara Bradley
35. Don and Patricia Bradley
36. Steve and Darlene Bradley
37. Isaac and Mae Bradley
38. Doris and Cleve Ed Bradley
39. Cleve and Lana Bradley

40. Henry Selby (widower of
    Anna Bradley Selby)
41. Silas and Dorothy Bradley
42. Pete and Mavis Daley
43. Don and Carol Smith
44. Hank and Pearl Bradley
45. Hobart and Liz Wilson
46. John and Helen Wilson
47. Bob and Sally Johnson
48. Rufus and Gloria Bradley
49. James and Rosemary Duncan
50. Joan Bradley (widow of
    R. C. Bradley)
51. Lloyd Hanson

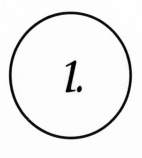

INTRODUCTION

We're All Kin

Residents of the rural, East Tennessee neighborhood called the top of the mountain often describe and talk about their neighborhood in terms of kinship. With the exception of a family of four who recently moved to the neighborhood from Virginia, all of the mountain's 198 residents are related, and people make much of this fact in remarking upon their social world. They are fond of explaining, for example, that "We're all at least a little bit kin," that "We're all one big family here"; and they stress this feature in comparing their neighborhood with American communities outside the mountains. Ties of kinship are evoked in numerous contexts as commentary on diverse facets of the neighborhood's social organization. Thus, a man explaining his land holdings may refer to his kin relationships with the owners of adjacent tracts or tell of how his great-grandfather settled the property in the nineteenth century. And he may explain a neighbor's church affiliation with, "Well, her daddy was one of the first preachers in that church," or remark of another neighbor that "ever since he married that Cooley girl, he's been going over there to Mountain Baptist." His manner of speaking suggests that relations of kinship, persons' positions in the neighborhood's kin network, are major determinants of social roles and group memberships.

All this is reminiscent of the classic kinship societies that have long preoccupied anthropologists, societies that are each organized on the basis of one or another of the many ordering possibilities inherent in a genealogy. Yet from another perspective the top of the mountain is anything but a kinship society. In fact it could even be argued that kinship plays a smaller role in the day-to-day lives of residents of the mountain than it commonly does for people in most other parts of the United States. This conclusion is suggested by the logic of the situation. As residents so often remark, everyone (or almost everyone) in the neighborhood is kin to everyone else. But where everyone is kin and where, as in most of American society, the indigenous conception of kinship neither includes principles for the categorization of kin into discrete and bounded groups nor even clarifies egocentric classifications beyond the range of first cousins, kinship would appear to be relatively meaningless as a basis for social action.

And indeed, although residents frequently use the terminology of kinship in speaking of their social world, the mountain's major social groupings—churches, communities, and even the neighborhood's four large extended family groups—often seem to be based on principles of organization and recruitment that are radically different from those of kinship. That is, social relationships and groupings are frequently spoken of as though they owed more to individual strategies and decisions based on a variety of personal considerations than to any discernable logic or principle of kinship. For example, while ancestry, which is viewed as a biological determinate, is said to play a major role in shaping residence patterns and therefore in determining the membership of the neighborhood's four communities, where a person lives is also said to be a matter of free choice, and residence histories reveal that this choice is in fact exercised often.

What, then, do residents mean in stressing the social im-

portance of kinship, of the fact that "We're all kin," a circumstance that—if viewed in terms of the usual anthropological
understanding of kinship as pertaining to relationships determined by ties of blood or marriage—often appears to have
very little relevance to their daily lives? It is with this problem
of the indigenous conception of kinship and the relation of
this conception to the social order of the top of the mountain
that this study is concerned.

The Background of Studies in Appalachia

Appalachia has long been considered to be a major "problem area" of the United States. Very possibly, this notion has
served to define Appalachia as a region, indeed has helped to
create "Appalachia" more than has any clear perception of a
shared and distinctive regional subculture.[1] It has, further,
strongly influenced Appalachian regional and community
studies, which seem animated less by an interest in culture
and society in the region than by a concern with identifying
those aspects of regional culture that can serve to illustrate,
define, or explain Appalachian problems. This section reviews
this perspective and discusses the dominant vision of an Appalachian culture that has emerged from it.

Many early writers treated Appalachia in terms of the influence of natural environment. In 1899 William G. Frost de-

[1] The definition and character, indeed the reality, of an Appalachian
subculture are problematic. Good discussions of topics related to this general issue are Henry D. Shapiro, *Appalachia on Our Mind: The Southern
Mountains and Mountaineers in the American Consciousness, 1870-1920* (Chapel
Hill: Univ. of North Carolina Press, 1978); Allen Batteau, "The American
Culture of Appalachia," paper presented at the American Anthropological
Association Meetings, Cincinnati, Nov.-Dec. 1979; and by the same au-
thor, "Appalachia and the Concept of Culture: A Theory of Shared Mis-
understandings," *Appalachian Journal* 7, No. 1-2, Special Issue, "Process,
Policy, and Context: Contemporary Perspectives on Appalachian Cul-
ture" (Autumn-Winter 1979-80), 9-31.

scribed the region of the Southern Mountains as "the mountainous backyards of nine states," which "as a place for human habitation . . . has one characteristic—the lack of natural means of communication." Frost attributed the region's distinctive character—which he described as marked by a cultural backwardness or "Rip van Winkle sleep"—to this geographically imposed isolation. "They have been beleaguered by nature," he explained.[2]

Closely echoing the words of Frost, Ellen Churchill Semple wrote that "the whole civilization of the Kentucky mountains is eloquent to the anthropogeographer of the influence of physical environment, for nowhere else in modern times has that progressive Anglo-Saxon race been so long and so completely subjected to retarding conditions."[3] Similarly, Arnold Toynbee argued in a notorious passage in *A Study of History* that the "inordinately severe" conditions of the mountainous environment of Appalachia have promoted a relapse into a kind of "neo-barbarism."[4] Analogous observations highlighting the role of the natural environment in shaping the character and problems of Appalachia, although not necessarily as deprecating as those quoted here, are found in the writings of many other early students of the region.[5]

While early writers dwelt upon the role of geography in setting Appalachia apart physically and culturally from the rest of the nation, later students have often sought to analyze the region and its problems in economic terms, arguing that certain features of Appalachia's economy—particularly that of the coal mining industry—have played a major role in mold-

[2]"Our Contemporary Ancestors in the Southern Mountains," *Atlantic Monthly* 83 (March 1899), 311.

[3]"The Anglo-Saxons of the Kentucky Mountains: A Study in Anthropogeography," *Geographical Journal* 17 (June 1901), 623.

[4]*Vol. II* (2nd ed.; London: Oxford Univ. Press, 1935), 312.

[5]For example, Horace Kephart, *Our Southern Highlanders* (1922; rpt. Knoxville: Univ. of Tennessee Press, 1976); John C. Campbell, *The Southern Highlander and His Homeland* (1921; rpt. Lexington: Univ. Press of Kentucky, 1969); S. S. MacClintock, "The Kentucky Mountains and Their Feuds," *American Journal of Sociology* 7 (July, Sept. 1901), 1-28, 171-87.

ing the character of society and culture in the mountain area. This orientation is apparent, for example, in the writings of Harry Caudill, who suggests that the mining industry has "undermined the character and independence" of the Appalachian people,[6] and in the work of Edward E. Knipe and Helen M. Lewis, who write that "coal mining created a system of 'peasant-like' structures over the traditional Appalachian culture."[7] For these authors, the region's social and cultural character and problems are to be ascribed less to the mountains than to the mining interests that have for long dominated its economy.

The writers noted have focused on establishing the degree to which problematic characteristics of culture and society in Appalachia ("a system of 'peasant-like' structures," a "Rip van Winkle sleep," and so forth) have been formed by externally imposed conditions and constraints of geography or economy. Another approach to the study of Appalachia—one that informs, to varying degrees, a large number of recent studies in the region[8]—reverses or confounds the terms of this casual relationship. Its general features are explained by Rupert B. Vance as follows:

---

[6]*Night Comes to the Cumberlands: A Biography of a Depressed Area* (Boston: Little, Brown, 1962), xii. Similar observations and arguments appear throughout Caudill's numerous published articles and his other widely read major work, *My Land Is Dying* (New York: Dutton, 1973).

[7]"The Impact of Coal Mining on the Traditional Mountain Subculture," in *The Not So Solid South: Anthropological Studies in a Regional Subculture*, ed. J. Kenneth Moreland, Southern Anthropological Society Proceedings, No. 4 (Athens: Univ. of Georgia Press, 1971), 25.

[8]Representative major works that I think exhibit the influence of this approach include Marion Pearsall, *Little Smoky Ridge: The Natural History of a Southern Appalachian Neighborhood* (University: Univ. of Alabama Press, 1959); Jack E. Weller, *Yesterday's People* (Lexington: Univ. of Kentucky Press, 1965); Thomas R. Ford, ed., *The Southern Appalachian Region: A Survey* (Lexington: Univ. of Kentucky Press,1962); John D. Photiadis and Harry K. Schwarzweller, eds., *Change in Rural Appalachia: Implications for Action Programs* (Philadelphia: Univ. of Pennsylvania Press, 1970); John B. Stephenson, *Shiloh: A Mountain Community* (Lexington: Univ. of Kentucky Press, 1968).

The older regional study was more concerned with causation
than with social change. It looked back to physical conditions
and limitations; and . . . it moved forward to describe insti-
tutional adjustments and the attitudes of the people and their
local leaders . . . In a study like the present we come to a point
where we find it hard to distinguish between cause and effect.
If we devote attention to religion in the mountains, we find
not only that it is an effect of the conditions under which
people have lived, but also that it operates either to change or
to perpetuate these conditions. Isolation, which begins as a
physical limitation enforced by distance and rugged terrain,
becomes mental and cultural isolation that causes people to
remain in disadvantaged areas and to resist the changes that
would bring them into contact with the outside world. The
effect of conditions thus becomes a cause of conditions, but
the new cause is an attitude, not a mountain. Since the mountains are not likely to be moved, we proceed on the assumption
that men can be moved.[9]

The "new regional study" suggests that Appalachian culture
and society is best approached not through the analysis of the
molding influence of environment or economy, but rather
through an understanding and appreciation of the deeply in-
grained values, attitudes, and beliefs that guide and render
comprehensible the behavior of the people of the region. Although they are often described as having originated as responses to early conditions of isolation or economic
dependence, these values are thought to have taken on an
enduring and independent life of their own. Called "individualism," "traditionalism," "religious fundamentalism," "familism," "fatalism," and so on, they are much the same
distinctive and defining features discussed often by Caudill,
Knipe, Lewis, and the earlier writers. Here, however, they
receive more concerted attention and emerge as both cause
and effect of present social and economic conditions.

[9]"The Region: A New Survey," in *The Southern Appalachian Region*,
ed. Thomas R. Ford, 8.

The approaches to the study of Appalachia outlined above differ from one another in their views pertaining to the causal relationships between environment, economy, and culture. They are all similar, however, in that they are shaped by an overriding implicit or explicit concern with relating society and culture to poverty, to "backward" conditions, and to economic and political marginality. When Frost, for example, wrote in 1899 that the Appalachian people have been "beleaguered by nature," he was offering an explanation not so much for the culture of the region as for what he thought was wrong with it.[10] And Caudill, Knipe, and Lewis discuss the economics of coal mining less as keys to understanding Appalachia than as keys to understanding its problems. Similarly, many writers who stress the role of values and beliefs present "individualism," "familism," "fatalism," and so forth as cultural traits that both arise from and perpetuate conditions of poverty.

Clearly, studies that illuminate the nature and causes of Appalachian problems are legitimate and indeed sorely needed; and many of the insights of Caudill, Knipe, and Lewis, for example, are important contributions to our understanding of the social and economic constraints faced by the poor in many parts of the region. Too often, however, I think the "problem area" approach introduces biases and distortions that do a grave injustice to the people of Appalachia.

These biases and their effects are most pronounced in many of the studies informed by the perspective that Vance calls the "new regional study," a perspective often labelled cultural because of its stress on attitudes and values. The inadequacies of this kind of approach in explaining the persistence of poverty (including its tendency to uncritically place the onus of responsibility on the poor themselves) have been discussed at

---

[10]The intellectual and political background of Frost's "invention" of Appalachia in his 1899 article is discussed in Shapiro, *Appalachia on Our Mind*, 113-32.

length in the social scientific literature[11] and will not be reviewed. Of concern here, rather, is the nature of the culture that emerges from these studies.

By no means are all cultural or new regional studies in Appalachia immediately concerned with explicating the causes of poverty in the region. Nevertheless, most appear to be shaped by the notion that the region is somehow "backward," for they, like cultural studies of Appalachian poverty itself, tend to focus on a limited set of patterns or traits that not only are explained as adaptations to conditions of poverty or deprivation but also are implicitly or explicitly equated with "culture."

These traits are usually called "values," "value orientations," "attitudes," and "beliefs." It appears—although the literature is not altogether clear on this point—that most writers who adopt this approach are seeking to explain patterns of behavior by means of values and beliefs. "Values" are, according to John Photiadis, "predispositions to action,"[12] and people act as they do in part or largely because of the values and beliefs they hold. The presence of these values is sometimes established by means of questionnaire surveys.[13] More

[11]With reference to Appalachia, see, for example, Dwight Billings, "Culture and Poverty in Appalachia: A Theoretical Discussion and Empirical Analysis," *Social Forces* 53 (Dec. 1974; rpt. Bruce Ergood and Bruce E. Kuhre, eds., *Appalachia: Social Context Past and Present* [Dubuque, Iowa: Kendall/Hunt Pub., 1976], 130-38); Helen M. Lewis, "Fatalism or the Coal Industry?" *Mountain Life and Work* 46, No. 11 (Dec. 1970), 4-14; Stephen L. Fisher, "Victim Blaming in Appalachia: Cultural Theories and the Southern Mountaineer," in *Appalachia: Social Context Past and Present*, ed. Ergood and Kuhre, 139-48. Good general discussions and critiques include Eleanor Burke Leacock, ed., *The Culture of Poverty: A Critique* (New York: Simon and Schuster, 1971); Charles A. Valentine, *Culture and Poverty: Critique and Counter-Proposals* (Chicago: Univ. of Chicago Press, 1968); Review of Valentine, *Culture and Poverty*, in *Current Anthropology* 10 (April-June 1969), 181-201.

[12]"Rural Southern Appalachia and Mass Society," in *Change in Rural Appalachia*, ed. Photiadis and Schwarzweller, 5.

[13]Ibid.; also, Thomas R. Ford, "The Passing of Provincialism," in *The Southern Appalachian Region*.

often, however, their presence and influence is established by pointing to the behavior they supposedly cause. Thus, for example, Appalachian people are said to be averse to participating in organized groups and activities (through which, it is assumed, they could further their uplift) because of the predisposing influence of a value of "individualism," which manifests itself in the reluctance of people to participate in formal organizations.[14]

Logical inconsistencies of this nature do not derive from the shortcomings of a cultural approach but rather from the frequent failure of these analyses to attempt seriously to confront the culture of the area or community under study and thus to provide a viable framework within which particular values, beliefs, or behavioral regularities can be apprehended. The emphasis is on selected fragments of belief rather than general principles or concepts.

A major criterion for this selection appears to be the degree to which these traits differ from those of an often idealized middle-class United States culture and thus serve to establish the singularity (and, usually, the deficiencies) of an Appalachian subculture. The frequently stressed Appalachian beliefs, values, and value orientations attributed to the Appalachian population or to segments of it are often described and defined by means of direct comparisons with their presumed middle American counterparts. Thus, for example, Marion Pearsall, Jack E. Weller, and John B. Stephenson all define the "present," "existence," or "shortened-time" orientation of Appalachia largely through contrasts with the "future" or "progress' orientation of middle-class Americans.[15] Usually little attention is devoted to the relationships between this present orientation and such other frequently noted Appalachian value traits as "familism," "traditionalism," and "individualism." And mention is seldom made of Appalachian values that do

---

[14]Weller, *Yesterday's People*, 29-31.
[15]Ibid., pp. 161-63 and chart on p. 6 attributed to Marion Pearsall (p. 5); Stephenson, *Shiloh*, 93-96.

not happen to be different from those thought to prevail in middle America. As a result of this selectivity, a picture emerges of a very truncated and fragmented Appalachian culture composed of a number of tenuously related traits, all of which rather perversely inhibit the movement of the region into the mainstream of United States society.

Described in terms of an assortment of cultural fragments closely associated with conditions of poverty, culture in Appalachia often emerges as an inchoate and emotional response to deprivation. Nowhere is this effect more apparent than in many of the writings on religion in the region, which have tended to interpret symbolic action in church settings primarily as a cathartic safety valve. Commenting on the emotionalism that often marks religious services in Southern Appalachia, Weller says,

> A "good" revival service with a lively evangelist, enthusiastic singing with heart-rending special music, perhaps accompanied by a guitar, and group prayer where all the faithful gather at the front and pray aloud at the same time can create an atmosphere of tense expectancy. Soon some will "get happy" and begin "speaking in tongues," as the service provides release for people who have been pent up in the midst of an incredibly dull life. The explosions of emotion which occur in the loud shouting and convulsive crying bring release to many who have no recreations, no social outlets, and no creative work to do it for them.[16]

Weller's perspective is echoed in Nathan L. Gerrard's analysis of the Holiness churches of Appalachia: "We suggest that the rural Holiness churches are viable because they serve to alleviate anxieties generated by status deprivation, guilt, illness, and last but not unimportantly, they supply recreation in areas of the region where recreational facilities are scarce."[17]

Because they are treated primarily as emotional responses

[16]Weller, *Yesterday's People*, 131-32.
[17]"Churches of the Stationary Poor in Southern Appalachia," in *Change in Rural Appalachia*, ed. Photiadis and Schwarzweller, 109.

to conditions of poverty, those features of religion in Appalachia—emotionalism, fatalism, rejection of formal ritual in favor of spontaneity, and other-worldliness, for example—that are usually stressed by students of the region are often viewed as being characteristic also of the religions of the many other peoples of the world who are economically disadvantaged. Pearsall, in her description of religious life in the East Tennessee neighborhood of Little Smoky Ridge, is quite explicit on this point:

> The values affirmed by the group—treasures in heaven, no need to "read a sweet word here on earth," nothing worthwhile "down here in the mirey clay," the sinfulness of worldly pleasures, the importance of ecstatic religious states, and the necessity for preaching the Bible "from lid to lid"—are common to many sects that have special appeal for the socially, economically, or emotionally impoverished of the world. They fit present conditions.[18]

Religion in Appalachia, and Appalachian culture in general, although invariably depicted as sharply contrasting with that of middle America, thus becomes indistinguishable in its major features from those of other groups who are similarly thought to be marginal to or alienated from society and who so appear to share in a widespread but rather amorphous "culture of poverty."[19]

It is undoubtedly true, as Pearsall suggests, that poverty plays some role in shaping many characteristics of the religions of "the socially, economically, or emotionally impoverished of the world," and, as Weller and Gerrard maintain, that these religions provide emotional and recreational releases for the poor. But religions, those of the rich and poor

[18]Pearsall, *Little Smoky Ridge*, 113-14.

[19]This phrase and the approach it represents is most closely associated with the work of Oscar Lewis. See, for example, his *Five Families: Mexican Case Studies in the Culture of Poverty* (New York: Basic Books, 1959); *La Vida: A Puerto Rican Family in the Culture of Poverty—San Juan and New York* (New York: Random House, 1966); "The Culture of Poverty," *Scientific American* 215 (1966), 19-25.

alike, not only address economic conditions and serve to make
life more bearable—they also make it more meaningful. Dickson D. Bruce, Jr. makes this point forcefully in his critique
of what he terms the social view of nineteenth-century southern frontier camp-meeting religion:

> Where such an exclusively social view falls short . . . is in its
> failure to take the explicitly religious content of the camp-
> meeting as seriously as it might, for it tends to lead one to
> characterize the camp-meeting as merely a social event with
> a religous veneer. While pointing to the emotional quality of
> the camp-meeting, this approach often leads one to neglect to
> specify what religious symbols made the emotional appeals
> work. Noting the sensational quality of conversion, those who
> focus on the social importance of the meeting often fail to
> make clear what one was converted from or to. Yet such ques-
> tions were crucial to frontier believers.[20]

Bruce's criticisms are apposite to many studies of religion
in contemporary Appalachia. For in focusing on the relationship between conditions of poverty and religious beliefs and
practices, students of the region have tended to neglect an
exploration of these religions' distinctive visions of the world
and the relationship of these visions to their wider socio-cul-
tural milieu. As a result, religion in Appalachia too often appears to be little more than a primitive reflex, largely devoid
of meaningful content and subtle symbolic associations. The
various sects and denominations of the region are said, for
example, to be "other-worldly."[21] But what does this mean
to members of an Appalachian mountain church; is not their
other-worldliness somehow distinctive and therefore crucially
different from the other-worldliness, say, of a Hindu *sanny-
āsin*? What are the "promises of the future life"[22] which moun-

[20]Dickson D. Bruce, Jr., *And They All Sang Hallelujah: Plain-Folk Camp-
Meeting Religion, 1800-1845* (Knoxville: Univ. of Tennessee Press, 1974),
7.
[21]For example, Gerrard, "Churches of the Stationary Poor," 105.
[22]Weller, *Yesterday's People*, 132.

taineers look forward to, and what relationship does their particular vision of the future life bear to their experience of life on earth? Such questions are seldom addressed.

Studies of religion in Appalachia, like those of the region's culture and society in general, have too often focused on selected fragments rather than on culture or religion. Of course no study, however voluminous, can ever depict and analyze the religion or culture of any group in its entirety. Some selection must be made. But this selection should ideally be guided by the particular categories, emphases, perspectives, and internal dilemmas of the culture under study as well as, inevitably, by the categories and concerns of the observer. Cultural studies that implicitly or explicitly treat Appalachia narrowly as a "problem area" and tightly structure their inquiries accordingly often serve only to mask cultural richness and complexity so that in the end the culture itself, reduced to a few nonadaptive traits, appears to be the problem.

The Setting of the Present Study

As will be seen throughout the following account, the top of the mountain bears numerous similarities to neighborhoods in many parts of Appalachia that have been described in terms of the theoretical frameworks discussed above. My concern here, however, is neither with the explication of Appalachian problems nor with exploring regional and poverty-related cultural patterns through the lens of a small neighborhood or area. It is, rather, with understanding aspects of the social and cultural organization of one small neighborhood located within the area commonly designated as Appalachia.

This neighborhood is situated on and about three narrow ledges or "flats" near the summit of one of the Cumberland Mountains in "Baker County," Tennessee, a section of the Cumberlands officially opened to settlement in 1805, following the signing of the second treaty of Tellico with the Cherokees. The Cumberland terrain in this area is characterized by precipitous slopes, narrow valleys, and rushing streams, and it was probably not inviting to most early travelers. Settlers accordingly trickled into these mountains slowly, most arriving only after the better lands immediately to the east, in the Great Tennessee Valley, had been taken up. The date of arrival of the first settlers on the top of the mountain is not known precisely, but fragmentary land titles, oral histories, and genealogies indicate that homesteads had probably been established in the neighborhood by around 1840. As the topography of the area suggests, conditions were inimical to farming, transport, and communcations; and the early years following settlement were perforce marked by an economy of relative self-sufficiency based on small-scale, diversified agriculture.

By the end of the nineteenth century, the top of the mountain's period of isolation had come to an end, for the neighborhood was by then caught up in the area's coal mining boom. Beginning in the closing decades of that century, agents for large land companies toured the mountains purchasing extensive tracts of land. With these purchases the commercial exploitation of the mountains' mineral and timber resources began: the timber was quickly cut over, railroads were built into the mountains, numerous large and small mines were opened, and a number of large boom towns and mining camps sprang up. The top of the mountain did not become one of the coal camps or company towns for which so much of the Appalachian coal region is infamous, but it did become a mining community in the sense that its residents sold much of their land to the land companies and turned from agriculture to mining as a primary source of livelihood.

Today coal is still extensively mined throughout the vicinity of the top of the mountain, but recent trends in the industry have greatly diminished its local economic importance. Coal is now more often extracted through capital-intensive surface mining than through labor-intensive underground operations, and even the remaining deep mines of the area are being increasingly mechanized. Mining employment has consequently declined dramatically. Many men of the top of the mountain, 63 percent of whom are experienced miners, continue to seek employment in the remaining local deep mines, but relatively few are currently employed in them. Although fourteen of the fifteen men of the neighborhood over the age of fifty-five were miners or were employed in mine-related jobs (high lift operator or coal truck driver, for example) prior to retirement, only sixteen of the forty-two men of age fifty-five or younger were so employed in 1976.

Due in part to the declining availability of mining jobs in the area and in part to changing aspirations, residents of the top of the mountain are increasingly seeking other kinds of employment. Few jobs are available in the immediate area, however, for the development of coal mining never led to further industrialization or urbanization in these mountains: the area is totally without manufacturing industries or commercial centers, and its social topography today comprises only a scattering of small rural neighborhoods and old, largely abandoned mining camps, most of which are not to be found on any map. To secure new employment, therefore, residents have had to turn outside the mountains, either moving away from the area or, if they wish to continue living on the mountain, seeking employment in the nearby towns and cities of the Great Tennessee Valley.

The top of the mountain is on the eastern edge of the Cumberland Plateau, only a few miles west of Walden's Ridge, which marks the boundary between the Cumberlands and the Great Tennessee Valley. Wide expanses of the Great Valley are visible from several vantage points on the mountain, and on a clear day one can see all the way across to the western slopes of the Great Smoky Mountains. The southeastern two-thirds of Baker County is in the Valley, an area of gently rolling hills and broad valleys and rivers. In contrast to the mountainous northwestern portion of the county, the Valley section is a socially and economically diversified area of agriculture, commerce, and industry containing five incorporated towns or cities with populations ranging from just over 1,000 to more than 28,000.

Until recently, residents of the top of the mountain were largely debarred from taking advantage of the diverse employment opportunities potentially afforded by the commercial and industrial centers in the Valley, for travel was difficult and people from the mountains often lacked the education and training requisite to urban jobs. A number of changes that occurred in the 1960s, however, have greatly reduced the physical and social isolation of the area. In that decade, telephone and electrical services were finally extended to the area, bringing with them radios and televisions. At about the same time, the neighborhood's two one-room schoolhouses were abandoned when children began to be bussed to consolidated elementary and high schools located in larger population centers. And many mountain roads, including the winding county highway that passes through the neighborhood of the top of the mountain, were graded and blacktopped, bringing the towns and cities of the county and of several adjacent counties to within easy commuting distance. The city of Knoxville, for example, is now about an hour's drive from the mountain, and the city of Oak Ridge, site of a major government laboratory, is about forty-five minutes away.

As a result of these kinds of changes, residents of the top of the mountain have numerous and growing contacts with the world outside the mountains through work, school, and travel. All children and young adults and some older adults have attended schools in the Valley or in more distant urbanized areas. About half of the mountain's 198 residents have lived off the mountain for at least a year, 37 outside the state. Many have worked or currently work in urban or small town businesses and industries as laundry employees, school custodians, motel maids, construction workers, assembly line workers, and so forth.

Many features of neighborhood life bear the imprint of these contacts. Almost all families have one or more automobiles or pickup trucks, and they own many of the other usual appurtenances of modern life: televisions, telephones, a variety of large and small appliances, and modern furnishings. National magazines and local newspapers are found in most homes, and national and regional political events and changing social mores animate many a discussion between neighbors. Favorite pastimes of the young include watching television, driving, and participation in such sports as baseball and basketball; and of their elders, watching television's soap operas and sporting events and participating in small, informal social gatherings such as baby showers and work parties.

Despite these contacts and similarities, however, the top of the mountain remains different in important ways from the average United States neighborhood. For example, although three residents of the mountain in 1976 were college graduates,[23] typical levels of formal educational attainment are low. Of the 115 residents who are over the age of eighteen, 93 or 81 percent lack a high school diploma, 30 of these having not completed the eighth grade and 16 having had less than six years of "school learning." For another example, unemployment is high. Most residents get jobs as unskilled or semiskilled workers, in positions that are often transitory, their occupants subject to periodic layoffs and abrupt dismissals. In 1976 twenty-eight residents were at least momentarily successful in finding work in the Valley. At the same time, however, 11 of the 42 men (26 percent) and 23 of the 39 women (59 percent) of the neighborhood aged eighteen to fifty-five were unemployed.

But employment and educational statistics, although indic-

[23]Since 1976 these three college graduates, all in their early 20s, have left the mountain. This pattern—of many of the talented young leaving the neighborhood permanently for employment elsewhere—has probably been prevalent for generations, and it is no doubt typical of rural neighborhoods and small towns throughout the United States.

ative of many differences between the top of the mountain
and average United States communities, do not capture many
of the most distinctive social and cultural characteristics of the
mountain, particularly those pertaining to the patterning and
nature of relationships among its residents.

Despite a long history of worker migration into the Baker
County area, dating from the early decades of the region's
coal mining era, most current residents of the top of the
mountain are the descendants, in one or more lines, of the
nineteenth-century settlers of the neighborhood. Most new-
comers to Baker County settled in the larger towns at the
edge of the mountains or in the large mining camps that dot-
ted the mountain area in the early part of this century. Outsiders, or people who had no kinship connection to residents,
seldom moved to the top of the mountain or to nearby small
neighborhoods except through marriage. And most marriages, including those of former mountain residents that I
was able to trace, were contracted with residents of the neighborhood or of the immediate mountain area of Baker and a
few adjacent counties. Moreover, many were with people to
whom some prior link through blood or marriage or both
was known or could be traced. As a result of these endogamous patterns and the infrequency of neighborhood in-mi-
gration by unrelated outsiders, the top of the mountain remains
a neighborhood composed predominantly of kinfolk. Although residents now have a variety of contacts that extend
outside their local area, their closest social relations—those of
daily interaction, mutual assistance, friendship, and still to a
large extent those of work—are formed within this kinship
network, with other residents and to a lesser extent with the
more distantly related people of surrounding, very similar
mountain neighborhoods. Close social relations are thus relations among kinfolk.

People of the top of the mountain dwell on these inter-
weaving links through descent and marriage and the close
social bonds associated with them when explaining and com-

menting on diverse aspects of their neighborhood. It is through these relationships that the neighborhood appears to be most clearly and meaningfully defined and shaped for residents. In the discussion of the mountain's social organization presented in the chapters that follow I will focus on exploring how this comes about and on explicating the senses in which kinship is socially meaningful and relevant on the top of the mountain.

Approach of the Present Study

This work explores an Appalachian neighborhood from a rather different perspective from those that have usually informed the study of communities in the region. Its starting point is not an idea of Appalachian shortcomings and problems but rather a recurring observation of the residents of this neighborhood, the top of the mountain, about their own social and cultural world—their observation that "we're all kin" and their sense, conveyed in a variety of comments and contexts, that this fact is of considerable social importance.

Students of Appalachia have long stressed the importance of kinship and family in the region. They have written, for example, that Appalachia "was, and to a considerable extent still is, a familistic society,"[24] and that kinship "is the central organizing principle of social life."[25] Few, however, have chosen to explore the subject in detail.[26] In what sense is Appa-

[24]Harry K. Schwarzweller, "Social Change and the Individual in Rural Appalachia," in *Change in Rural Appalachia*, ed. Photiadis and Schwarzweller, 53.

[25]George L. Hicks, *Appalachian Valley* (New York: Holt, Rinehart and Winston, 1976), 35.

[26]Among these exceptions are Elmora Messer Matthews, *Neighbor and Kin: Life in a Tennessee Ridge Community* (Nashville: Vanderbilt Univ. Press, 1966); Allen Batteau, "Modernization: Inflections on the Appalachian Kinship System," unpublished paper; James Stephen Brown, "The Conjugal Family and the Extended Family Group," *American Sociological Review* 17 (1952), 297-306.

lachia a familistic society, and how does kinship organize social
life—by what mechanisms and into what patterns? It is precisely because kinship and families are of such seeming importance that the meaning of these terms should be explored
carefully and in what way they are important should be
specified.

In the chapters that follow, some of the social and cultural
significance of the fact that "we're all kin" on the mountain
is discussed in analyses of the three kinds of social groupings—
"families," "communities," and "churches"—that residents
regularly distinguish above the level of the nuclear family or
the household. Each of these groups is often described as
though it were based, to varying degrees and in different
ways, on bonds of kinship. Thus, the mountain is organized
into four extended family groups, said to be composed of the
descendants and affines (spouses and their relatives) of the
descendants of four founding ancestors who settled on the
mountain in the mid-nineteenth century. Similarly, while residents of the neighborhood's four communities often speak as
though their choice of residence were unencumbered by kinship, the land of each community is said to be "family land"
that was acquired and settled by these ancestors and subsequently "passed on in the family" for generations. Most of
the residents of each are accordingly members of the same
family, that one founded by each community's first settler.
And although the churches of the neighborhood are on the
one hand open "to all who would believe" regardless of family
or community affiliation, they are also frequently discussed
as though each were associated with a particular family.

As is evident from these brief remarks, the memberships
of families, communities, and churches are largely cotermi-
nous. The Bradley family, the community of Bradley Flats,
and the Baptist church located in Bradley Flats, for example,
all comprise, by and large, the same people. But families,
communities, and churches are nonetheless conceptually distinct. Residents' comments on the family groups of the neigh-

borhood stress the notion of ascription by birth and of descent
from a common ancestor. Communities, on the other hand,
are residence groups, and although family bonds are thought
to play a major role in determining where an individual resides, residence, unlike family affiliation, is explicitly said to
be a matter of individual choice. And while church membership, like community residence, is thought to be ultimately
based on the individual's decision, relationships among members of the congregation are in some ways likened to those
ideally prevailing among family members.

It is suggested that the different principles embodied in residents' notions pertaining to families, communities, and
churches derive from and inform the indigenous conception
of kinship. That people of the top of the mountain emphasize
kinship and, as will be seen, invest it with not inconsiderable
cultural elaboration suggests more than that they value kinship
relations above all others or that their notion of "your first
duty is to your kin" shapes much of their behavior. These
kinds of points have been stressed in numerous studies of
neighborhoods in Appalachia, but on the top of the mountain,
where almost everyone is kin in many overlapping ways, notions of general and unspecified family relations and duties
logically would seem to be relatively insignificant to the patterning of the neighborhood's social organization. And in stat-
ing that "we're all kin", people of the mountain are not just
reiterating an obvious fact. I suggest and will try to demon-
strate that they are, rather, making a highly condensed statement about their understanding of the nature of social
relationships on the top of the mountain, of what makes their
local society cohere.

It will be apparent to readers acquainted with the work of
David M. Schneider that this study owes much to the approach developed in his seminal work on American kinship.[27]

[27]*American Kinship: A Cultural Account* (Englewood Cliffs, N. J.: Prentice-Hall, 1968).

Sylvia Junko Yanagisako has recently written of the difference between Schneider's approach and the more usual treatment of kinship in the anthropological literature:

> As Schneider . . . has acutely noted, the past tendency for anthropologists to limit cultural analysis—that is, the analysis of culture as a system of symbols and meanings—to religion, ritual, magic, myth, and other presumably "expressive" spheres stems from a false dichotomization of institutions into "instrumental" and "expressive" domains. Because institutions like kinship appear to be based on objective realities (as for example, property, goods and services, birth, copulation, and death), most kinship studies have been concerned with analyzing the norms and social relations that organize these activities. . . . In contrast, the cultural analysis of kinship focuses upon the symbolic and meaningful structures underlying the normative and behavioral systems of kinship. Its goal is the identification of the cultural units of kinship as these are defined and differentiated by the natives themselves and the explication of the system of symbols and meanings that these units form.[28]

Thus, departing from the received notion that kinship necessarily pertains exclusively to the social and biological facts of consanguinity and affinity, Schneider maintains that kinship is itself a cultural construct.

While the present study does not by any means neglect the social aspects of kinship, it follows Schneider in focusing on the cultural significance of kinship, of the fact that on the mountain "we're all kin," and attempts to treat kinship as a cultural rather than an exclusively social and biological phenomenon. Not surprisingly, since the top of the mountain is an American neighborhood, many of my findings and conclusions closely parallel those of Schneider for American kinship in general, particularly certain aspects of his discussion of the American conception of kinship as compounded of an

[28]"Introduction," Special Section: American Kinship, *American Ethnologist* 5 (Feb. 1978), 1.

"order of nature" and an "order of law." Yet I also depart from Schneider's analysis and approach in many ways and am throughout considerably less faithful to his acocunt than to the statements of the people of the top of the mountain. This is as it should be, of course, for what kinship is "all about," according to Schneider, is whatever the "natives" say it is all about.[29]

[29]"What Is Kinship All About?" in *Kinship Studies in The Morgan Centennial Year*, ed. Priscilla Reining (Washington, D. C.: Anthropological Society of Washington, 1972).

2.

FAMILIES

Family Founders

Residents of the top of the mountain relish discussing the divers circumstances of the local settlement of four men, the founders of the mountain's four large extended family groups. Interest in the subject is keen, and whenever exact knowledge is lacking or deficient, debate and speculative theories abound.

It is widely known that the first Campbell was a certain Isaiah Foley Campbell hailing from Foley Bottom, a small community near the southeastern foot of the mountain. Isaiah and his family probably settled on the mountain sometime shortly before the Civil War when, it is believed, Isaiah purchased about seventy-five acres of land on one of the upper "flats" from the non-resident owner of a large land grant.

The next arrivals were Robert Johnson and his wife and children from Sourwood Grove, another small community situated at the southeastern foot of the mountain. Robert Johnson traded his property in Sourwood Grove for about one hundred acres of mountain land owned by a resident named Isaiah Wiley. Some say that the Johnsons came to the mountain before the Civil War, citing as evidence the wartime death of one of the sons, Isaac. Others, pointing out that this proves nothing about the Johnsons' place of residence at the time, maintain that the Johnsons must have settled on the mountain after the war because they know that their daughter Hannah was born in 1865 in Sourwood Grove.

Whatever the exact date of the Johnsons' arrival, however, all agree that it was before 1871. This was the year in which, according to an old deed retained by a member of the Bradley family, Abraham Bradley of Sourwood Grove became the first Bradley to settle on the mountain when he purchased two hundred acres of land from a local settler named Zachary Wiley.

Last to arrive was one Hiram Johnson who is said by some to have been "some kin" to Robert Johnson, although the precise nature of the genealogical link is not generally known. Others contend that Hiram and Robert Johnson were not related at all. Most residents do not know where Hiram lived before he came to the mountain, but he and his family settled on a ledge or flat below Abraham Bradley's land, and his descendants live there to this day.

While some facets of family history and ancestry are obviously topics that hold great interest for many, people seem to know and care very little about many other details of their ancestry. Residents appear to take little or no interest, for example, in their European heritage or even in the American experience of ancestors prior to their settlement on the mountain. Many aspects of more recent history are also neglected. Although most residents are aware, for example, that the Campbells, the two families of Johnsons, and the Bradleys were not the first people of European descent to settle on the mountain, they are generally unconcerned with the history of earlier settlers.

Knowledge of the Wileys—who sold land to both Robert Johnson and Abraham Bradley—is very limited and provides a striking illustration of the highly selective nature of mountain residents' historical interests. The Wileys were the contemporaries of the first Campbells, Johnsons, and Bradleys and were their predecessors on the mountain. Yet most people claim to know little of the Wileys beyond the fact that some persons bearing this surname once lived on the mountain and that they sold their land to the Johnsons and the Bradleys. Most who have thought at all about the matter suppose that the Wileys simply moved away shortly after Isaiah Wiley and Zachary Wiley "sold out" to Robert Johnson and Abraham Bradley.

There is much evidence, however, that indicates that this may not be what in fact occurred. The Wiley name appears in many of the records and documents—deeds, cemetery markers, family Bibles—pertaining to all four of the family groups of the top of the mountain, often in contexts that strongly suggest that all of the Wileys may not have left the mountain in the nineteenth century and even that descendants of Isaiah or Zachary Wiley may still be living there in the guise of Campbells, Johnsons, and Bradleys.

To describe two illustrative examples:

First, genealogical records contained in family Bibles belonging to some of the descendants of Abraham Bradley identify his wife as Sally Wiley Bradley. Since it is known that Abraham Bradley purchased two hundred acres from Zachary Wiley, it seems highly probable that the wife of Abraham Bradley was related to Zachary Wiley, possibly as a sister or daughter, and that many of the Bradleys may therefore be descendants or collaterals of Zachary Wiley. Descendants of Abraham and Sally Bradley who were questioned about the matter, however, were strikingly ignorant and uninterested, noting only that while it was possible that Sally Bradley had been "some kin" to Zachary or Isaiah Wiley, they did not know anything of her family background "for a fact."

The second example concerns the wife of Hiram Johnson. Like Sally Wiley Bradley, Hiram Johnson's wife—one Bessie Wiley Johnson—was also a Wiley before her marriage. Many residents of the mountain are aware of this fact, but most say they know little else about her. A few elderly descendants of

Hiram and Bessie Johnson, however, claim to be more knowledgeable, and they state with assurance that not only was
Bessie Wiley Johnson the daughter of Zachary Wiley but also
that the couple acquired their land in Mine Flats through inheritance from Bessie's father. Yet despite their belief that they
are descendants of Zachary Wiley and in contrast to their detailed knowledge about Isaiah Foley Campbell, Robert Johnson, Abraham Bradley, and Hiram Johnson, these residents
know nothing more about Zachary Wiley—his origins, the
circumstances and approximate date of his arrival on the
mountain, his relationship to Isaiah Wiley—and are seemingly
uninterested in the subject.

If it is true, as these examples suggest, that ancestors of
many of the people of the top of the mountain were residing
there before the arrival of Isaiah Foley Campbell, Robert Johnson, Abraham Bradley, and Hiram Johnson, why are these
other ancestors ignored? I submit that the history of the early
Wileys may be of little interest to residents because their story
obscures or contributes nothing to the conceptual differentia-
tion of the present family groups of the mountain. For while
the identity of the founders or "first" members of each family
and the subsequent history of these groups are quite clear to
mountain residents, this clarity is achieved, as will be seen,
only through a highly selective recall and interpretation of
historical and genealogical detail. Hence, though people know
rather a lot about the four men they consider to be the founders of their families, they know relatively little about ancestors
in general.

Families and Genealogies

Every resident of the top of the mountain, with the afore-
mentioned exception of a family of four who recently moved
to the neighborhood from Virginia, is considered to be a

member of one or the other (or, in a few cases, of two) of four large family groups. Each family is designated by a surname, and each is thought of as being composed of "close" kin who are the descendants and affines of the descendants of a male bearing the family name.

Everyone who is said to be "one of them Campbells" is thought to be descended from—or affinally related to the descendants of—Isaiah Foley Campbell, the "first Campbell on the mountain." Likewise, the members of the Bradley family are all "Bradleys or leastwise married to Bradleys," the descendants or affines of the descendants of Abraham Bradley. The other two family groups are both known by the surname Johnson and are distinguished from one another by affixing place names. Those people who consider themselves and are considered by others to be members of the family founded by Robert Johnson are "the Johnsons of Rocky Gap" or "the Rocky Gap Johnsons," while those tracing family relationships to Hiram Johnson are "the Johnsons of Mine Flats."

Most people's closest social relations are within the family group, among their close kin, and intra-family kinship links are staples of conversation on the mountain. The following excerpt from a tape recorded conversation between two residents illustrates the kind of context in which family relationships are often discussed:

> "You know, Eli and Alice went and got theirselves a lot of new [things]."
> "Yeah, I seen it. . . . They're always spending money, uh, buying new things, and don't have a cent put away. They've always been that way."
> "Yeah, but it's funny, ain't it, how the others is so different. Now you take Cal—he's so careful and don't hardly spend nothing. Must have a lot saved up by now. Funny how two brothers can be so different."
> "Well, Cal takes after his mother that way. She was old Sam's girl, and that bunch was always tight-fisted. And, 'course, you got to remember that Alice was a Smith [a non-resident family] and that comes into it."

A great deal of genealogical information is exchanged through such conversations, and most adult residents of the mountain can trace the relationships that link the members of their own family group to one another and to their family founder three to five generations ascendant. These relationships are depicted for each family group in Figures 1 through 4 below. (Only residents of the mountain in 1976 and connecting collaterals and ascendants up to and including the founding ancestor shown; large numbers of kin, living and dead, who "moved off" and left no descendants on the mountain are not included.)

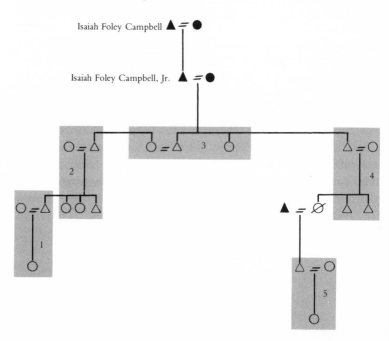

Figure 1. The Campbells. In this and in all subsequent genealogical diagrams, individuals enclosed in screened boxes are members of one household. Solid symbols represent deceased individuals, and slashed symbols represent non-residents who are included in the diagrams for the purpose of depicting connections among residents.

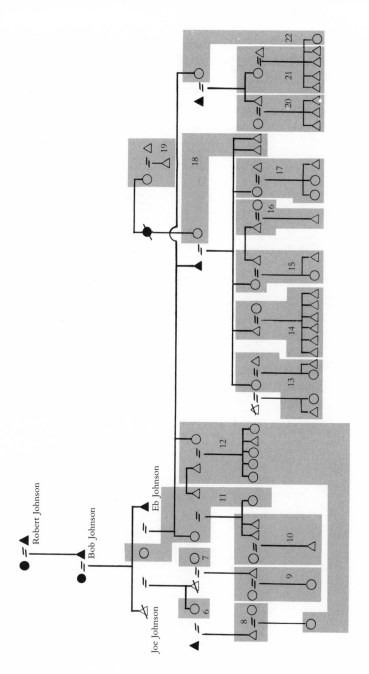

Figure 2. The Johnsons of Rocky Gap.

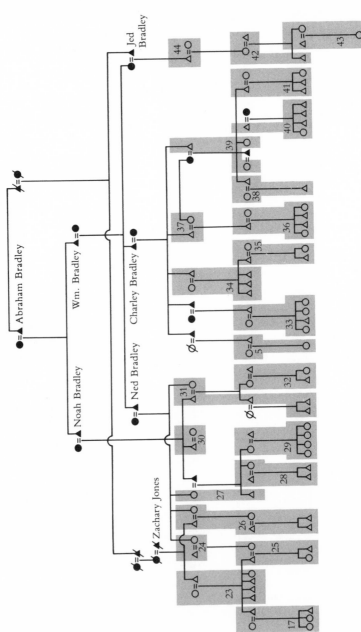

Figure 3. The Bradleys.

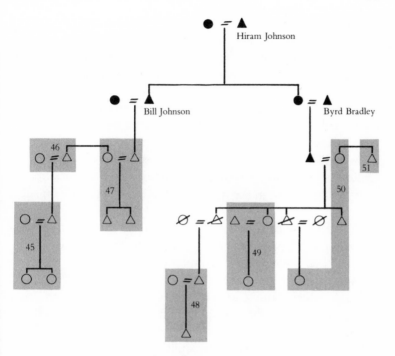

Figure 4. The Johnsons of Mine Flats.

These diagrams were constructed not by asking people to list the resident members of their own or the mountain's other family groups and their genealogical relationships to one another and the family founders but rather by listening to and recording conversations, explanations, and comments pertaining to residents' family affiliations. Statements about family group memberships are made both about individuals and households and can sometimes vary with context. Thus, the family affiliations of the members of Household 3 in Figure 1, composed of Luther and Mary Campbell and Luther's sister, Jane Campbell, are sometimes differentiated for individuals by noting that Mary was or is a Green, from a nearby mountain neighborhood; and they are also treated as a unit by referring to the entire household as Campbells. By extension,

Households 1 and 2, also in Figure 1, are sometimes differentiated as Greens from the other members of the Campbell family; and they are also spoken of as members of the Campbell family, to whom they are affinally related through Mary Green Campbell. Ignoring for the moment the double attributions of outside and mountain family group memberships to affinally related individuals and households, however, the cumulative result of residents' statements like "they're all Campbells" or "he's one of them Johnsons—Mabel (Johnson) Dalton's boy" is the genealogical delineation of the mountain's four family groups in the manner depicted in Figures 1 through 4.

Compared with their familiarity with the details of consanguineal and affinal relations among their close kin, or members of their own family group, most people are not highly conversant with the number and precise nature of all the ties through which family groups are related *to one another*, that is, through which the Campbells are related to the Bradleys, the Bradleys to the Johnsons of Rocky Gap, and so forth. These relationships between families generally are described as being "distant" ones. "We're all at least a little bit kin," as residents say, but some kin—namely, members of one's own family—are "close" kin, while others—members of other families—are "just a little bit kin" to oneself. Most residents are familiar with at least some of these inter-family links, but usually only with those that are recent or are closest to themselves. For example, any marriage between resident members of two of the mountain's family groups that had occurred, say, within the last twenty or thirty years would be a matter of common knowledge, and the members of the household concerned would either be spoken of as members of both family groups (as in fact is the case for Households 5 and 17, which are each accordingly depicted on two diagrams, Figures 1 and 3 and Figures 2 and 3) or would be affiliated with one family with the in-marrying spouse noted to be also, as an individual, a member of the other family group (as occurs in the case of Household 21, of the Johnson family of Rocky Gap, in which the husband is also said to be one of the Bradleys). With regard to a long past inter-family marriage, the grandchildren of the alliance will almost certainly be aware of their links to both family groups involved, noting for example that "My grandmother was a Johnson," but many other people may be unaware or only dimly aware of the link.

That most residents are not particularly knowledgeable about the details of all inter-family links is not to say, however, that these links are not knowable. Consultations with several elderly residents who are reputed to know all about the "old timey" days and who have old family Bibles on hand elicited many connections between family groups. One elderly former resident of the mountain, now residing in a nearby Valley town, has been engaged for some years in tracing the ancestry of one of the mountain's families. She generously shared her data with me, and they revealed many more inter-family relationships.

The results of these inquires are presented in Figure 5, which depicts consanguineal and affinal ties among all residents of the top of the mountain. Because of the difficulties of legibly diagramming large numbers of overlapping links, some of the more distant relationships among mountain residents have been omitted.

This figure reveals that genealogical relationships among all mountain residents (and not just among members of the same family group) are far more complex and close-knit than residents generally suggest to be the case. Thus, for example, Robert Johnson and Hiram Johnson and the two families founded by them are thought by most people to be distantly related through unknown ties or to be unrelated to one another. In fact, however, both families of Johnsons are descended from Robert Johnson, for as was recalled by two elderly residents, Hiram Johnson was Robert Johnson's son. Also noteworthy are the two second generation marriages among the children of Robert Johnson, Isaiah Foley Camp-

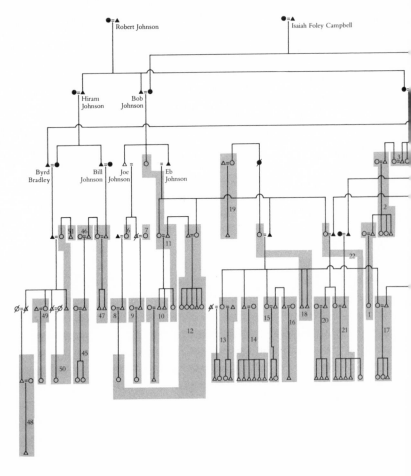

Figure 5. A Neighborhood Genealogy. For the memberships of households designated by numerals, see Key to Households, pp. *xv*.

bell, and Abraham Bradley, through which many mountain residents are descended from all of these men.

A number of older people are aware of these ties, and they point to them as evidence of the distant interrelatedness of the

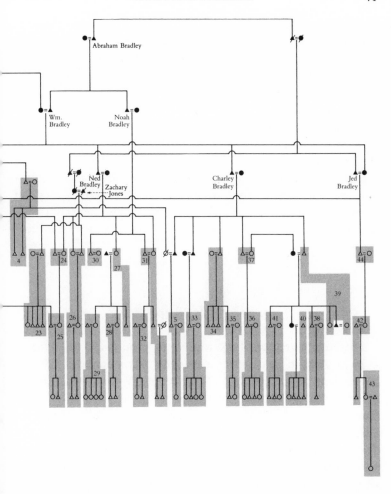

mountain's families. They do not, however, interpret them as suggesting that these family groups are each descended from several family founders or that most people are members of more than one family. Clearly, when residents speak of each family as being composed of "close" kin who are all "Bradleys or leastwise married to Bradleys" (or Campbells or Johnsons, as the case may be), and when they trace its origin to the arrival on the mountain of one and only one putative founder, they are lending each family clearer contours and a more distinct identity than it genealogically possesses.

More than this, they are thereby creating these families, for what Figure 5 depicts is not the genealogical relationships among four families but rather an endogamous soup from which four conceptually distinct family groups have been delineated through a process of selective recall and interpretation of genealogical detail.

But what principles and concepts have informed this selection and creation? How, to phrase the problem somewhat differently, does the indigenous image of the neighborhood as composed of four distantly related and distinct "families" come to be?

Some Possible Approaches

The family groups of the top of the mountain are each said to be and are in fact composed of the descendants and affines of the descendants of a founding ancestor. They are thus apparently similar (except for the promiscuous inclusion of affines) to the ancestor-focused cognatic or nonunilineal descent groups that anthropologists have described for many societies throughout the world. Indeed, Ward H. Goodenough illustrates one form of this kind of kinship system with the example of some Appalachian communities:

> In an endogamous community, the course of time will produce an increasing overlap of membership in such groups [nonunilineal descent groups], until eventually everyone is descended from all the founding ancestors and the several descent groups have become coterminous with the community itself. . . . Approximating this arrangement . . . are some of the valley communities of the Kentucky mountains . . . in which all persons accounted as members, as distinct from outsiders, must

have one parent who was accounted a member, and so on back
to the original settlers from whom all members are by now
equally descended.[1]

Like Goodenough's Kentucky mountain communities, the
neighborhood of the top of the mountain has a history of
numerous locally endogamous marriages. As a result, most
contemporary residents are the descendants (or affines of the
descendants) of more than one of the neighborhood's early
settlers. Unlike the overlapping descent groups described by
Goodenough, however, the memberships of the mountain's
four families are by and large discrete. To be sure, almost
every resident can, if desired, trace some kind of consanguineal or affinal relationship to every other person and to all
founding ancestors. Each therefore could theoretically claim
memberships in all four family groups, which would create
a situation similar to that described by Goodenough. The
point, however, is that residents either do not bother to trace
these links, or that when they do come up—as so often happens in conversations with a visiting anthropologist—residents do not interpret them as suggesting that they are
members of more than one family group. A member of the
Bradley family, for example, whose mother's father was a son
of Abraham Bradley and whose mother's mother was a
daughter of Isaiah Foley Campbell, is unlikely to say, "I'm a
Bradley through my grandfather and a Campbell through my
grandmother." He describes himself, rather, as simply a Bradley and acknowledges his relationship to the Campbells by
noting that "My grandmother was a Campbell." Despite,
therefore, the existence of a large number of known or knowable genealogical relationships between family groups, most
people view themselves and are viewed by others as being
members of only one family.

[1]*Description and Comparison in Cultural Anthropology* (Chicago: Aldine,
1970), 51-52. For his description of the organization of these Kentucky
communites, Goodenough cites an unpublished 1960 paper by Kutsche.

But how is it decided that a particular individual or household belongs to one family rather than another? For as by and
large discretely bounded groups, the families of the top of the
mountain must incorporate some rule or principle of closure
by which it is determined who, among all the descendants of
an apical ancestor, are and are not to be counted as family
members and which therefore informs the delineation of these
four families from the endogamous soup.

It is tempting here to posit the operation of a submerged
patrilineal principle. Although here as elsewhere throughout
Western culture kinship is traced through both males and fe-
males, it is nonetheless possible that family group membership, like surnames, is here inherited patrilineally. Indeed, the
fact that these families are known by surnames would seem
to suggest that this might well be the case.

Some of the genealogical data presented in Figures 2 through
5 can be construed as providing support for this hypothesis.
For example, most of the descendants of the second generation
marriages among the children of Isaiah Foley Campbell, Robert Johnson, and Abraham Bradley appear to have been assigned to the family group of the husband in these marriages.
Despite these prominent cases, however, the figures reveal
numerous instances in which family group membership is apparently based on relationships through women. Consider,
for example, households 48, 49, 50, and 51 (Figures 4 and 5),
who are descended from (or affinally related to the descendants of) Abraham Bradley in the male line but who are
counted as members of the Johnson family of Mine Flats
through Hiram Johnson's daughter, the wife of Isaiah Foley
Campbell's and Abraham Bradley's grandson. And, as these
latter cases illustrate, although each family is designated by a
surname, all persons who are included and include themselves
as, in these cases, "one of them Johnsons" do not necessarily
bear that surname. It seems that a patrilineal principle, if op-
erative, is often more honored in the breach than in the
observance.

A more arresting potential explanation of the principles underlying the determination of family group membership resides in the possibility that membership may be determined primarily or entirely on the basis of principles other than those of kinship. In other words, these "families" may not be kinship groups at all, or they may be only partly so, combining kinship and other principles of recruitment or exclusion.[2]

Anthropologists have traditionally thought of kinship relationships as being distinct kinds of social relationships, analytically different from those, say, of politics and economics, and they structure their studies accordingly. Hildred and Clifford Geertz, however, suggest that it may often be misleading to isolate the kinship component of multifaceted relationships: "What we would like to suggest . . . is that to start with the notion that there is an isolable, internally integrated system of 'sentiments,' 'norms,' 'categories,' to which the adjective 'kinship' can be unambiguously appended is not the most profitable way to go about the matter."[3] Starting from a kindred premise—that all "natives" do not necessarily share the dominant anthropological notions pertaining to the natures and proper categorization of social relationships—David M. Schneider arrives at a conclusion that is similar to but stated more radically than that of the Geertz's. He suggests that under these circumstances "kinship" may not exist at all, that it is "an artifact of the anthropologists' analytical apparatus" and that "like totemism, the matrilineal complex, and matriarchy, [it] is a non-subject."[4]

It is possible, then, that many relationships between kinfolk that anthropologists have traditionally discussed in terms of

[2]Indeed, Goodenough (*Description and Comparison*, 53) has pointed out that *all* restricted descent groups must apply some criterion of exclusion in addition to descent. Thus, patrilineal (and matrilineal) descent groups use the nonkinship criterion of sex to restrict membership. Traditionally, however, unilineal descent systems are the archetypal form of social organization based on kinship.

[3]*Kinship in Bali* (Chicago: Univ. of Chicago Press, 1975), 155.

[4]"What Is Kinship All About?" in *Kinship Studies*, ed. Reining, 59.

kinship categories and principles are shaped by concepts and
rules that do not involve kinship in an anthropological sense.
But if this conclusion is true for the top of the mountain, if
the four families residing there are not "really" kinship groups,
what are they?

One possibility is that they are local or territorial groups.
James S. Brown and Allen Batteau have each found that ter-
ritoriality is an important component in the organization of
Kentucky mountain "family groups" or "sets" which appear
to be very similar to the family groups of the top of the
mountain. According to Brown, "Family groups are typically
not only groups of close kin but also territorial groups. Often
the families constituting a family group lived in a cluster, each
family being closer to the other families in the family group
than to any other family—usually because they had inherited
parts of the same estate."[5] In Batteau's words, written twenty-
five years later, "The elementary unit of the kinship system
of the Mountain People of eastern Kentucky is the localized,
non-unilineal descent group. This unit . . . is constituted by
those descendants of an apical ancestor who reside at or near
the original homeplace of the ancestor. These *sets*, or family
groups as [Brown] has characterized them . . . are arranged
in a segmentary array."[6]

Brown's and Batteau's findings are in accordance with mine
for the top of the mountain, for most of the mountain's households that are said to belong to the same family group are
found to reside together in the same neighborhood section or
"community" on "family land" passed on from the family's
founding ancestor. It is clear, therefore, that community residence, land ownership, and family group affiliation on the
mountain are closely related, a subject that will be explored
in Chapter 3. For the present, however, it is sufficient to note

[5]"The Conjugal Family and the Extended Family Group," *American
Sociological Review* 17 (1952), 300.
[6]"Modernization: Inflections on the Appalachian Kinship System," unpublished paper, 1.

that residents of the mountain clearly distinguish between residence groups and family groups. The "community" of Mine Flats, for example, is described as being inhabited "mostly" by members of the Johnson "family" of Mine Flats. Thus, although the memberships of communities and families are known often to coincide, they are conceptually distinct groups.

Another possibility for characterizing and for understanding the family groups of the top of the mountain is brought to mind by a comment made by Schneider with reference to prescriptive alliance systems: "In principle a table of random numbers might be used to allocate new members to groups— and indeed, systems have been reported from New Guinea which work that way."[7] This suggestion, whether seriously intended or not, merits consideration, for the principle of random numbers accords very well with the actualities and "regularities" of family memberships on the mountain. An appropriate "rule" explaining the allocation of individuals to family groups, constructed on the basis of observed regularities, would be: All descendants and affines of the descendants of the founder of a family are members of that family except those who are members of other families.

Each of these briefly discussed possibilities—patrilineages, local groups, random clusters—has some merit, because each can account for at least some aspects of the family organization of the top of the mountain. They all share a serious problem, however. This problem is not that they cannot be used to explain all cases of family membership assignment—although most of them in fact cannot. It is, rather, that they seek to anchor the family groups of the top of the mountain in the empirical realities of statistical regularities while ignoring the cultural dimension of what they may mean to the people who, after all, have created and live within them. While it is possible to compose "rules" such as the one suggested above that adequately "explain" these family groups insofar as they restate

[7]"What Is Kinship All About?" in *Kinship Studies*, ed. Reining, 57.

their composition and character in terms of general principles, these principles cannot be said truly to underlie and inform their creation unless they somehow accord with the indigenous understanding that both derives from and shapes these families.

The Cultural Delineation of Families

Residents of the top of the mountain do not call their family groups patrilineages, communities, or random clusters nor do they describe them as being composed of people who are related to one another through males, or who live close to one another, or who perhaps "just happen" to belong to the same family. They call them, rather, "families," and they explain that each family originated with the local settlement of a family founder. Family members are "close" kin who are "all Campbells [or Bradleys or Johnsons] or leastwise married to Campbells," descendants and affines of the descendants of the family founder.

It is clear from much of what residents say of families, however, that family members are thought to be related to one another and to the family founder in more than a strict genealogical sense. Family members are not only described as the grandchildren or great-grandchildren of the family's founding ancestor, they are also said to "take after" him, to have inherited many of his personal characteristics. For example, the stories told of "old Hiram Johnson," founder of the Johnson family of Mine Flats, depict him as a colorful, rather picaresque character who often ran afoul of the law but who was nonetheless a likeable and good-hearted person. His descendants "take after" him in these respects, for the Johnsons of Mine Flats are considered by themselves and by others to be a fun-loving people whose high spirits often get them into trouble but who are friendly, loyal, and not at all malicious. In contrast, the Bradleys are characterized as a very industrious family whose members, except for a proneness to occasional sexual misadventure, are upright and respectable, and the stories told of Abraham Bradley and his sons highlight these traits.

Having inherited many characteristics from the founder, family members are therefore very similar to one another, and each family group is often spoken of as though its members all shared a common personality or set of family traits. The kinds of traits attributed to different family groups are diverse: generous, quick to take offense, God-fearing, law-abiding, upright, respectable, loyal, friendly, clannish, prone to violence, stuck-up, loud, selfish, untrustworthy, no-account. As might be expected, traits that are positively valued are most often emphasized in describing one's own family group while negatively valued traits are frequently stressed in talking of other families. Despite such differences in emphasis, however, there is considerable consensus in the attribution of traits to each family, and each is accordingly depicted as possessing a unique "personality" or configuration of characteristics that is shared to some extent by all its members.

The concept of the similarity of family members is sometimes carried to extremes. It is related, for example, that some years ago the Johnsons' (of Rocky Gap) oath was "thrown out of court" in the county courthouse because it was well known that members of this family would swear to anything in order to "cover for" and protect one another. As it happens this action was not taken against "the Johnsons," but against several individual members of the Johnson family. But in using this particular manner of speaking in telling this story, a manner suggesting that legal action can be taken against a "family" as such, residents depict a family group as a discrete and homogenous entity.

The similarities among family members are thought to be "naturally" or genetically determined, based on the shared "flesh and blood" inherited from the family founder. Family traits are said, for example, to "run in the family," and people frequently support such statements by pointing to the evidence of the same or similar traits in the family founder. Residents appear to believe, moreover, that the sharing of flesh and blood has important implications for the nature of social relationships obtaining among kinfolk. People who share the same blood and are hence very similar to one another are also considered to be naturally "close" to one another, united by bonds of mutual love, trust, and support. "Blood is thicker than water," and the relationships between parents and children, brothers and sisters, uncles, aunts, and cousins are thought to be compelled by blood, by the immutable biological nature of human beings. A mother loves her child, for example, not simply because she chooses or is morally expected to do so, but also because it is in her nature to do so. Likewise, family members love and support one another not simply because it is in their interest to do so or because of some cultural or moral imperative, but also because of a natural and biological imperative, one that derives from the fact that they are all very like one another, that they are all one flesh and blood.

Not all family members, of course, are of one flesh and blood, for as residents note, many family members are related to the others through ties of marriage rather than consanguinity. But while affinally related family members are distinguished from other members as in-laws in some contexts, they are also said to share many of the family traits. This is because "like marries like"—people are thought to have a natural tendency to marry those who are most like themselves. (Indeed, many people of the mountain have married relatives, sometimes members of their own family group, which validates for residents the truth of their conceptions.) Thus affines—spouses of family members and their relatives—tend to be viewed as sharing many of the family characteristics even if they are not known to be related to the family founder. Their likenesses, although not based on biological inheritance from the founding ancestor, are nonetheless "natural" in the sense that they derive from inborn traits and predilections.

In the indigenous view, then, a family is a "natural" group of "close" kinfolk who are said to be very like one another and united by social bonds of mutual love and support. These similarities and social bonds are thought to be naturally determined, however, and are expressed in terms of genealogical relationships, for the closer people are genealogically, the more similar and socially and emotionally close they are said to be. In the case of consanguines, these relationships are expressed and explained through the notion of shared flesh and blood inherited from a common ancestor, the family founder. In the case of affines who are not also known to be consanguines, they are also thought to be largely natural, residing in the individual's inherent and immutable make-up and resulting from the fact that like marries like.

But in the real world genealogical proximity and social and psychological closeness do not always coincide. Kinfolk, however, closely related they may be, do not always have similar or even compatible personalities and do not always love or even like one another. How are these facts reconciled with the notion of a family as a group of closely related people who are very like one another and who accordingly love and support one another?

Individual differences, far from threatening the concept of the unity of the family group, are often cited as proof of its essential oneness and family-like character. Although residents stress the fundamental similarity of all family members, they also pride themselves on their individuality and on the ability of all family members to get along together or at least to "put up with" one another's idiosyncracies. It is said that among kinfolk each person is treated as an individual. While people must conform to social conventions in relationships with non-kin, they can "be themselves" with their close kin, who will love them despite and sometimes even because of their faults. This is implied in the saying that kinfolk "stick together through thick and thin." Thus, while love among family members is founded upon an identity, it often endures despite—and even encourages—difference.

Sometimes, however, this individuality threatens the solidarity and amity that is supposed to pervade family relationships. It may then be said of a person that he or she is "not really a Bradley." As this statement suggests, this kind of difficulty is often resolved by the "distancing" of individual kin through terminological variation or simple denial of kinship.

However, the top of the mountain also exhibits a more thorough-going resolution of this problem through the organization of the neighborhood into four family groups. Individuals who are not "really" members of one family are, as it often happens, members of other families. Let us consider, for example, the case of Larry Bradley of Household 21 (Figures 2 and 5), a great-great-grandson of Abraham Bradley. Larry's father, now deceased, was much disliked by many of the Bradleys—he was, as the saying goes, "not really a Bradley." His son Larry is married to Tula Dalton Bradley, a great-great-granddaughter of Robert Johnson, and the couple and their children reside in Rocky Gap and have little to do with the Bradleys. When speaking of Larry Bradley as an individual, members of the Bradley family either acknowledge (albeit grudgingly) that he is a Bradley or qualify this by pointing out that he, like his father, is "not really a Bradley." When speaking of the household as a unit, however, people unambiguously assign Larry and Tula Bradley and their children to the Johnson family of Rocky Gap. Thus, kinship connections through the wife have been stressed while those through the husband have been largely ignored—not as a function, for example, of a matrilineal bias but rather as an interpretation of existing social relationships.

As this case vividly illustrates, the family groups of the top of the mountain, while based on genealogies, are also more than genealogical groups. When people on the mountain talk

about one another as members of particular families and not
of others and when they trace the origin of each family to a
founding ancestor, they are not seeking to provide themselves
and others with a neighborhood genealogy. They are rather
talking about social relationships among residents. But they
are not simply employing an idiom of kinship and descent to
characterize relationships that are really of some other nature.
For it is thought that these relationships *are* kinship—they are
"natural" similarities and bonds, believed to result from a
common biological heritage or to be expressed through
marriage.

A family is thus composed of those kinfolk who are both
genealogically and socially close and who invest their relationships to one another with cultural significance, tracing
their descent and the social bonds that are believed to result
from this to a common family founder. Clearly, all the descendants of a family founder are not necessarily members of
the family group said to have been founded by him, for all
kinfolk do not behave as family to one another. But, as seen,
genealogical relationships on the mountain are so complex and
interwoven as to permit considerable latitude in the interpretation of family group memberships and contours. Indeed, it
is this very complexity that, far from constituting a barrier to
the demarcation of relatively discrete family groups, actually
facilitates the creation of families that confirm and conform
to ideas of what a family is.

Cultural Process and Family Histories

It is possible to infer from the above discussion that individuals simply select those kinship ties they would like to
emphasize and in this way affiliate with the family group of
their choice. But while this undoubtedly captures much of the
process through which family membership contours are

shaped, it neglects the indigenous view of families as natural groups rather than voluntary associations. A far more satisfactory and illuminating interpretation is suggested by the circumstance of two cases of dual family membership.

As noted earlier, members of two households—those of Fred and Grace Bradley (Household 5) and of Jed and Sally Jones (Household 17)—are depicted in the diagrams as belonging to two families, the first to the Campbell and the Bradley families and the second to the Johnson family of Rocky Gap and the Bradley family. Fred Bradley's mother, now residing elsewhere, is a daughter of Seth Campbell and a great-granddaughter of Isaiah Foley Campbell; while his father, now deceased, was a great-grandson of Abraham Bradley. Fred and his wife Grace are on close terms with both the Campbells and the Bradleys and are considered to belong to both family groups. Similarly, Jed and Sally Jones maintain close ties with many of the Johnsons of Rocky Gap, to whom they are related through Sally, who is the great-great-granddaughter of Robert Johnson, and with the Bradleys, to whom they are related both through Jed's paternal grandmother and through several contemporary affinal links. This household is accordingly described by residents as belonging to both the Bradley family and the Johnson family of Rocky Gap.

It is possible that these ambiguities of family contours will eventually be resolved by the children of these two families somehow opting for exclusive membership in one or the other of the family groups to which they are currently considered to belong. But the process through which family groups are created may perhaps be better understood in terms of shifting images rather than shifting people. That is, current images of the family groups of the top of the mountain may themselves undergo gradual alterations that would continually account for and resolve recurring discrepancies and ambiguities.

To illustrate, fifty or one hundred years hence, residents of the top of the mountain may not conceive of their neighborhood as composed of four families known as the Campbells, the Johnsons of Rocky Gap, the Bradleys, and the Johnsons of Mine Flats. For example, the neighborhood may by then be viewed as consisting of three families—the Bradleys, the Johnsons, and the Joneses. Under these hypothetical circumstances, the Bradley family group would be composed of the descendants only of some of the people currently considered to be Bradleys but would encompass the descendants of the group now known as the Campbells. The children and descendants of Fred and Grace Bradley would belong to this group. The Johnson family would consist of the descendants of the present Johnsons of Mine Flats and the descendants of some but not all of the Johnsons of Rocky Gap. And the Joneses, to which group the descendants of Jed and Sally Jones would belong, would include the descendants of some of the present members of the Bradley family plus the descendants of some of the people who are now included among the Johnsons of Rocky Gap.

This example, while not offered as a prognostication, is neither far-fetched nor randomly chosen. Both the Campbell family and the Johnsons of Mine Flats are very small groups that have lost many members through death and out-migration and are therefore possibly likely to become conceptually united with other families. And families may not only shrink and then disappear through mergers with other groups, they may also grow and, their memberships inevitably becoming increasingly heterogeneous, eventually be thought of as two or more families. Both the Johnsons of Rocky Gap and the Bradleys have become very large families, and their future conceptual division is not altogether unlikely.

From the perspective employed in this illustrative discussion, the processes through which family groups are delineated are best understood not only as boundary shifts resulting in part from the vagaries of individual social alignments, but also as shifting family group identities, cores, or foci through which these vagaries are continually re-interpreted. They are both social processes involving changing affiliations of individuals with family groups and cultural processes involving the changing conceptual definition of these groups. Indeed, from this perspective family groups as social units become inseparable from the ideas that both inform and are informed by them.

That indigenous concepts of the identities of family groups may evolve and change in the manner suggested above is supported by historical evidence. As discussed in the opening pages of this chapter, it is quite probable that the Wileys who lived on the mountain in the nineteenth century did not all move away from the mountain as residents suppose. Rather, some of them may have intermarried and eventually been conceptually merged with several of the mountain's present family groups. Other evidence of past alterations of family group contours is provided by the history of what was once known as the "Wilson family." The Wilsons, consisting at one time of five or six households, used to live high above the forebears of the Campbells, Johnsons, and Bradleys almost on the literal top of the mountain, but according to residents they "moved off" several years ago. As it happens, however, all the Wilsons did not move far, for a few married with the Johnsons of Rocky Gap and the Johnsons of Mine Flats and only "moved off" as far as these communities. Yet "the Wilsons" no longer exist as a family group, those Wilsons who still reside on the mountain having become parts of what are now the Johnson families of Mine Flats and Rocky Gap.

This view of the mountain's families as fluid, shifting groups, which is suggested by these histories and by the earlier discussion of hypothetical future family configurations, sheds light on at least one problematic aspect of the history of the Campbells, Johnsons, and Bradleys. As noted earlier, it appears that the descendants of the early marriages among the children of Isaiah Foley Campbell, Robert Johnson, and Abraham Bradley were in each case eventually assigned to the family groups of the sons of these men, an observation that hints of the operation of a patrilineal principle, which is seemingly ignored, however, in many other cases. But this is a retro-spective assessment that assumes residents of the mountain have always conceived of their family groups as "the Camp-bells," "the Johnsons of Rocky Gap," "the Bradleys," and "the Johnsons of Mine Flats." It is more likely, from the per-spective suggested here, that at the time of these marriages and for some time thereafter these groups had not yet emerged as separate families. Under this assumption, any apparent pa-trilineal bias becomes only an artifact of contemporary family group contours and of a tendency to trace the ancestry of each through males and male surnames whenever possible.

The continual redefinition of family group identities and family founders does not of course occur at random. People do not simply choose their families and ancestors, and pro-cesses of family group delineation are always shaped and con-ditioned by the givens of genealogical history. It is suggested, however, that these processes are also creative of this history. It is not strictly accurate to describe the mountain's families as groups composed of the descendants of an apical ancestor, for this firmly embeds these groups in an inalterable genea-logical process that began in the nineteenth century. More satisfactory would be: each family group traces its descent to an apical ancestor. For Isaiah Foley Campbell, Robert John-son, Abraham Bradley, and Hiram Johnson did not begin their careers as family founders. Rather, they became so in retrospect through the conceptual organization of the past in a manner that lends meaning to the present.

COMMUNITIES

Family Land

Coming into the Cumberlands through Coal Gap, an old mining town about twenty-five miles northwest of Knoxville, the highway follows the floors of narrow valleys for the first twelve miles or so, passing by scattered clusters of small houses, mobile houses, one- or two-room churches, and combined gas stations and general stores. Twice the traveler passes through larger crossroad communities. The first, Brownville, is about four miles southwest of Coal Gap and is another old mining town. It has a small health center (which Seth Campbell, a resident of the top of the mountain, was instrumental in establishing), an elementary school (which is attended by the children from the top of the mountain), a community center, a small restaurant, two general stores with gas stations, three churches (Holiness, Methodist, and Southern Baptist), and about 150 homes. The second, Sourwood Grove, about eight miles further to the southwest, is the community where both Robert Johnson and Abraham Bradley lived before they settled on the top of the mountain; it has one Southern Baptist church, a community center, a combined general store and gas station, and about seventy-five homes.

After passing through Sourwood Grove, the highway begins a steep and sharply winding ascent: on the right the
mountainside rises abruptly; on the left is an almost sheer
drop. No homes are encountered until reaching the neighborhood of the top of the mountain, about four highway miles
up from and to the northwest of Sourwood Grove.

To the uninitiated, the neighborhood of the top of the
mountain presents a scattering of homes and a few barns,
churches, and cemeteries. They cluster around a short stretch
of the county highway near the summit of the mountain and
extend out for one to two miles along gravel or dirt side roads
on three narrow benches. The talk of residents lends the
neighborhood landscape a more elaborate social topography,
however, for people there speak of four separate residential
areas or "communities" known as Campbell Flats (sometimes
also called Laurel Woods), Rocky Gap, Bradley Flats (or Cherokee Bluff), and Mine Flats (or Lower Bluffs, or Johnson
Flats). As is suggested by the custom of naming communities
after families ("Campbell Flats," "Bradley Flats," and "Johnson Flats") and of identifying families by means of place names
("the Johnsons of Rocky Gap" and "the Johnsons of Mine
Flats"), each family is associated with and dwells predominantly within a particular community.

Figure 6 illustrates the general locations of these four communities and the family group affiliations of each of their
households. As can be seen in the diagram, most members of
the Campbell family reside in Campbell Flats, located at the
southern end of the bench lying south of the county highway.
Similarly, the communities of Rocky Gap, straddling the
highway in an elevated pass, Bradley Flats, on a second bench
north of the highway, and Mine Flats, on a third bench be-
neath Bradley Flats, are each inhabited mainly by members
of the Johnson family founded by Robert Johnson, the Bradley family, and the Johnson family tracing descent from Hiram
Johnson.

According to residents, members of a family group tend to

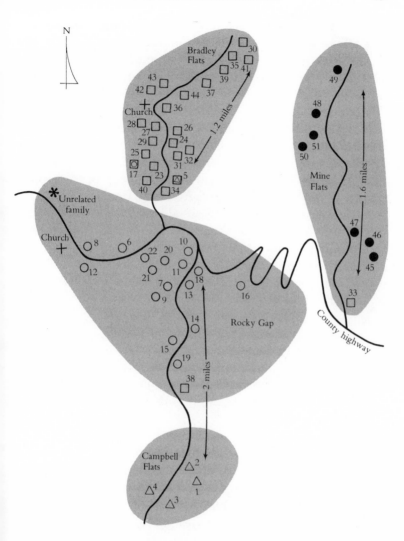

Figure 6. The Communities of the Top of the Mountain. For identification of households, see Key to Households, pp. *xv*. Squares represent households belonging to the Bradley family, circles represent the Johnsons of Rocky Gap, triangles represent the Campbells, and solid circles represent the Johnsons of Mine Flats.

live together in the same community because each community
was settled by one of the founders of the neighborhood's four
family groups. Campbell Flats was settled by Isaiah Foley
Campbell when he purchased about seventy-five acres there
in the mid-nineteenth century. Isaiah's land was subsequently
"passed on in the family" to his descendants and heirs, members of the Campbell family, who consequently live there to
this day on land that is considered to be "what you might call
family land." In the same fashion, the communities of Rocky
Gap and Bradley Flats are situated on the properties once
owned by Robert Johnson and Abraham Bradley, lands that
were also passed on to their descendants, the members of the
Johnson family of Rocky Gap and the Bradley family. Although all the land of Mine Flats was sold to a land company
in the early twentieth century, the descendants of Hiram Johnson continue to reside there on land that they too consider to
be their ancestral property:

> No, we don't own this here land. It was sold to the land
> company way back. We lease it from the land company. . . .
> Don't know how many acres. . . . Don't none of us own this
> here land—land company's got it all. But we got rights to it,
> see. Us Johnsons been living here ever since old Hiram John-
> son came here, so we all got lifetime leases from the land
> company.

Thus, family members reside together in the community
settled by their forebears because the land of each has always
been "passed on in the family." This land is in each case
thought of as "family land" to which family members have
moral if not always legal title by virtue of their descent from
the individual who settled the area in the nineteenth century.

Residence

The notion of "family land" that has been retained in the
family for generations suggests residential stability and con-

tinuity. Yet the population of the top of the mountain is rather mobile. Of the neighborhood's 198 residents, 97 have lived outside their present communities for one or more years, 37 of these outside the state. Of the 52 households in the neighborhood in 1976, 18 had resided in their present house for less than five years. Some of these households are young couples and their children who often move into and out of the neighborhood as they look for work and change jobs. Others are older people who have settled recently on the mountain after many years of moving about the region, often following the mines.

The residential history of one of Abraham Bradley's great-granddaughters, Sarah Bradley, describes a pattern typical of many people on the mountain: in 1934 at the age of twenty-two, Sarah Bradley married Riley Bradley, her father's father's brother's son, also of Bradley Flats. Sarah and Riley were at that time unable to obtain a home of their own in Bradley Flats, so for the first four years of their marriage they lived in the community of Rocky Gap, where they leased a vacant house and a few acres from the land company owning the area bordering the locally owned property of that community. In 1938 Riley took a job in Virginia, and Sarah and Riley moved to a mining camp there. When the mine closed in 1940, they returned to the mountain and lived for a year with Sarah's parents in Bradley Flats while they looked for a home of their own. They then returned to the house in Rocky Gap where they had spent the first years of their marriage. Sarah and Riley lived there for about four years until, unhappy with life in Rocky Gap ("folks wasn't real friendly there"), they moved to Isaac's Creek, a small community about three miles away, at the western foot of the mountain. They found, however, that they did not care for Isaac's Creek either, so after one year they returned to Bradley Flats. There they moved into a recently vacated house that Riley owned jointly with his siblings. Later, in 1950, Sarah's father gave the couple six acres of his land in Bradley Flats, and they built a house in which Sarah, now widowed, resides to this day.

As Sarah Bradley's history indicates, individual preferences, changing employment opportunities, the availability of land and houses, and so forth often can play major or decisive roles in determining where a family resides at any time. Thus, people have stayed in or moved to their communities for a variety of practical and personal reasons:

> They moved up here from Foley Bottom 'cause their trailer got shot up twice down there.
>
> I've always lived here. Guess I'm just too lazy to try anywhere else.
>
> We came here a few years back. . . . Bradley Flats is a good place to live 'cause you can raise hogs here, and you can't do that lots'a other places where you always got your neighbors breathing down your neck.
>
> I wouldn't live down there in Mine Flats if they paid me. That road's always a mess in the winter and tears up your car something terrible.

Clearly, while community residence is often spoken of as a function of inherited and enduring family "rights" to the land, where a particular individual or household lives is also frequently explained in very different terms suggestive of alternatives, deliberation, and chance. The neighborhood's residence patterns thus emerge as both determined by family rights to ancestral lands, and therefore seemingly immutable, and as governed by the changing needs and decisions of a mobile population.

Land Ownership and the Passing On of Family Land

Although the people of the top of the mountain sometimes move and travel about often, they are also "mountain" or

"country people" who use the land to raise a variety of crops
and animals. Although the neighborhood has not relied on
agriculture as a primary source of livelihood since the opening
of numerous coal mines throughout the area in the nineteenth
century, many residents plant gardens of corn, potatoes, beans,
okra, tomatoes, cabbage, and summer squash and raise chick-
ens, hogs, and occasionally cattle. A few cultivate small or-
chards, keep bees, or grow sugar cane for molasses. Of the
neighborhood's fifty-two households, thirty-two engaged in
one or more of these pursuits in 1976, and approximately
sixty-seven acres were devoted to agriculture and animal
husbandry.

Yet many people are not land owners. Of 404.3 neighborhood acres owned by current or recent residents, 373.5 are
owned individually or jointly by only twenty-two people,
with average holdings of seventeen acres. Fourteen individuals
or couples with average lots of 2.2 acres own the remaining
30.8 acres, and twenty-eight households are landless. Although the land of the neighborhood is "family land" to which
all family members "got rights," clearly all family members
do not have equal rights to it.

Many residents' present landless circumstances are known
to have resulted from property sales to land companies, most
of which took place in the early decades of this century. The
eight households of Mine Flats, four of which are the direct
descendants of the early owner Hiram Johnson, all now live
on leased company land. And the company land fringing
Rocky Gap and Bradley Flats hosts seven landless households
of these communities.

Much of the ownership concentration of the acres remaining in residents' hands is due to the vagaries of family birth
and migration rates, small families like the Campbells having
sizable individual holdings and large families like the Johnsons
of Rocky Gap having small lots. It is known to result in large
part, however, also from parental reluctance to relinquish control of any land, offspring often acquiring no family property

until their parents are aged or deceased. Fourteen of the mountain's twenty-eight landless households are composed of the children and grandchildren of land owners who have not yet passed on any of their property. Many parents fear their young married children will move on soon and sell their property to others. Although they encourage their children to live close to them, they often provide them only with permission to park a mobile home on part of their lot pending evidence of the young couple's decision to really settle down. These trial years are often very prolonged, however, and many middle-aged couples who have lived most of their adult years in the neighborhood still own no land and live on parental property.

Most land owners do eventually provide at least some of their children with land, either by default—dying intestate—or by willing it to them, or by giving or selling it, often in their very old age, to those of their children who have stayed on the mountain. Many currently landless households of the neighborhood, therefore, will probably become land owners in the future. All these future acquisitions are by no means a certainty, however. Parents commonly—and, it is thought, rightfully—take many factors into account in their deliberations about giving or selling property to their offspring. These include the differing needs and plans of their various children and, inevitably, their different feelings toward each. People who are estranged from their parents or who seem likely to move away, for example, may be disinherited.

The circumstances under which people may not inherit, and which often contribute to the concentration of land ownership in a few hands, also relate significantly to residents' brisk trade in real estate. Many people, rather than simply holding their land in trust for the next generation, buy and sell property among a wide range of kin and even occasional outsiders. As one result, people who eventually obtain some of their parents' property often receive tracts different from those passed on to their parents from their grandparents. Of the mountain's twenty-four land owning households, only fourteen acquired their present property from the parents of one of the spouses, and in six of these cases this parental land had originally been purchased from people other than the grandparents. As another result, moreover, some people may receive no land at all from parents who decide to sell all their property to others. Ten of the twenty-eight landless households descend from people who once owned land on the mountain but sold out without passing any on to their lineal descendants.

In most cases, land that is "sold off" is nonetheless still retained "in the family," for most land transfers occur between close kin, members of the same family group. Mountain residents' proclivities both for buying and selling land and for keeping it in the family are illustrated by the ownership history of a 61.2 acre tract near the southern end of Bradley Flats. According to an old deed retained by one of the Bradleys, this parcel was once owned by Robert Johnson and was sold in 1896 to Robert Bradley, a son of Abraham Bradley. In the 1920s Robert Bradley (who left no descendants on the mountain and is not included in the genealogical diagrams in Chapter 2) decided to move away from the mountain, and he sold the property to his nephew Ned Bradley, grandson of Abraham Bradley.

Shortly after the death of his first wife in 1944, Ned remarried and left the mountain, it is said because his new wife and his adult children did not get along. Ned needed cash at this time, so he sold tracts of 20 and 17.2 acres to two of his daughters and sons-in-law—Marj and Cal Jones and Lucy and Pete Dalton—who were willing and able to give him "a good price."

When Ned separated from his second wife in 1952, he returned to the mountain to live in his former house, which he still owned, with his youngest daughter and son-in-law, Lucy and Pete Dalton. In 1954 at the age of 69, he realized (according to some of his children) that should he die intestate his

land would pass in trust to his second wife, with whom he
was not on speaking terms, and on her death be inherited
jointly by his thirteen children by his two marriages. Ned
therefore "deeded" his remaining twenty-four acres to his four
daughters and sons-in-law who lived on the mountain, giving
three couples—Lizzie and Bob Bradley, Marj and Cal Jones,
and Sarah and Riley Bradley—six acres apiece and giving
Lucy and Pete Dalton, who were caring for him in his old
age, six acres plus his house, the "home place."

While Ned Bradley retained and eventually conveyed by
sale or gift all of his land intact to four of his children, his
daughters and their husbands have not all followed his example. Within a few years of Ned's death in 1965, Lizzie and
Bob Bradley decided they did not need all of their six acres
and sold three to Lucy and Pete Dalton, whose own land was
conveniently adjacent. Shortly thereafter, Marj and Cal Jones
decided to move to a small town outside the mountains and
sold their twenty-six acre tract (twenty acres purchased from
Ned plus six acres that Ned had later given to them) to Cal's
brother and sister-in-law, Eli and Alice Jones, who had for
some years been interested in moving to Bradley Flats from
the small community at the foot of the mountain where they
then resided. Marj and Cal concluded after a year, however,
that "city life" was not for them and decided to return to
Bradley Flats. Alice and Eli Jones were unwilling to give up
any of their new property, so Marj and Cal prevailed on
Marj's sister and brother-in-law, Lucy and Pete Dalton. This
couple felt that it was "only right" that Marj and Cal should
have some of the property that had once belonged to Marj's
father Ned and accordingly sold them 2.7 of their 26.2 acres
(17.2 acres purchased from Ned Bradley, 6 acres that he had
given them, and 3 acres purchased from Lizzie and Bob Bradley) and assisted them in building a new house on the property.

Thus, Ned Bradley's 61.2 acres came to be apportioned
among four of his children and their in-laws as follows:

Marj and Cal Jones	2.7acres
Lucy and Pete Dalton	23.5
Sarah and Riley Bradley	6.0
Lizzie and Bob Bradley	3.0
Eli and Alice Jones	26.0

Some of these couples are now beginning to pass on their land to their own children. To date, Sarah Bradley, now widowed, has given tracts of one half and one acres to two daughters and their husbands, Nora and Luther Hamilton and Cleta and Dave Randolph, because, Sarah says, these two couples have decided to reside permanently on the mountain and also because she feels particularly close to them. Similarly, Alice and Eli Jones have given .8 acres to a son and daughter-in-law, Jed and Sally Jones; and Lucy and Pete Dalton have given one acre to a daughter and son-in-law, Frances and Houston Jones (son of Alice and Eli Jones). Also, several years ago Lizzie and Bob Bradley sold one acre to a daughter and son-in-law. But the younger couple later decided to move, and when Bob Bradley declined to buy the property back from them, they sold the property to Lucy and Pete Dalton, who of course owned the adjoining tract. Later Bob Bradley changed his mind, and Lucy and Pete Dalton, considering the property rightfully to belong to the first couple despite Bob's vacillations, resold it to them for the purchase price plus the interest paid on a bank loan they had taken out to acquire the property.

Currently, the 61.2 acres that Ned Bradley purchased from his uncle and later sold and deeded to four of his children is divided among nine households composed of his children, his grandchildren, his children's in-laws, and their children:

Sarah Bradley	4.5 acres
Nora and Luther Hamilton	.5
Cleta and Dave Randolph	1.0
Lucy and Pete Dalton	22.5

Frances and Houston Jones	1.0
Alice and Eli Jones	25.2
Jed and Sally Jones	.8
Marj and Cal Jones	2.7
Lizzie and Bob Bradley	3.0

A schematic diagram of the land transfers resulting in this
distribution is provided in Figure 7.

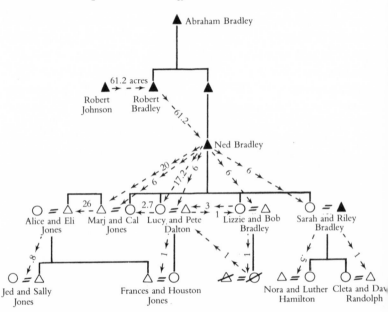

Figure 7. Ownership History of a Tract of Land in Bradley Flats.

As this history illustrates, land is often retained in the family
despite numerous sales and subdivisions. Although land owners are not constrained to sell their land to close kin, they
often choose to do so for a variety of reasons. For example,
family members may be willing to offer a better price than
others because they have a sentimental attachment to the land
or because they own adjacent tracts. Also, residents have more
frequent contacts with their close kin than with others and

therefore may know of more prospective buyers among close kin than among people they see only occasionally.

Perhaps of greater importance than these considerations, however, is the belief that giving or selling land "in the family," among those with whom one has close ties and among those who are considered to have ancestral rights to the property, is "the right thing to do." Doing the right thing is not only a source of personal satisfaction, it also enhances one's social standing and prestige in the community. Lucy and Pete Dalton, for example, are highly respected in Bradley Flats in part because of their unselfish land sales to Marj and Cal Jones and to Lizzie and Bob Bradley. Similarly, a number of other neighborhood residents have acquired reputations for fairness and generosity by renting or selling land to relatives in need of a home or by donating or loaning land to the entire community, for example, in one case for the expansion of a local cemetery and in another for a community baseball field.

The pattern that emerges from these transactions is seemingly similar to that described by Elmora Messer Matthews for a Middle Tennessee community. It is, she says, "sort of an extended and untimed 'fruit basket turnover' " in which "the same families change places often but continue to fill the positions" with the land remaining "generation after generation within the same valley lines."[1] Individual residents of the mountain buy and sell land often, and these transfers are known to be influenced by many kinds of circumstances—offers from prospective buyers, children's plans and intentions, financial need, and so forth. But decisions pertaining to the disposition of property are also influenced by considerations of the rights and duties associated with family ties, by the belief that family members have rights to the land of their ancestors. As a result, the family land of the top of the mountain, although often not passed directly from generation to generation and although not shared equally by all family members, seems usually to

[1]*Neighbor and Kin*, 13-14.

have remained "in the family," and most people live on or own land in the community settled by and inherited from their family founder.

Family Rights and Individual Rights

It is said on the mountain that family members have rights to the family land in the community settled by their forebears and that children have rights to the property of their parents. It is also asserted, however, that individual owners have the right to dispose (or refuse to dispose) of their property whenever and in whatever way they wish, a right that can be and, as seen, is exercised in many ways. The notion that neighborhood land is both ancestral family property that should rightfully be passed on to each new generation from the older one and personal property, the disposition of which depends (again, rightfully) on the discretion of individual owners, has not infrequently been a fertile source for neighborhood discord and resident dissatisfaction. For while present residence and land ownership patterns are in many respects in keeping with the general notion that the land of each community is family land that has always been passed on in the family, they do not always accord in details with all residents' ideas that they all have undefined but nonetheless important rights to their ancestral property.

For example, the current unequal distribution of family land has recently become a subject of controversy among the Johnsons of Rocky Gap. The dispute concerns a tract of fifty-seven acres that once belonged to Bob Johnson, son of Robert Johnson. Bob Johnson died intestate in 1921, and his property was jointly inherited by his children, who soon legally divided it among themselves in accordance with an agreement that allotted each an equal share. As the years passed, however, his children and grandchildren bought, sold, and traded portions of this property among themselves, and the original fifty-seven acres came in this way to currently consist of seven separately owned tracts of 20, 16.5, 10.8, 4, 2.2, 2, and 1.5 acres. Some members of the Johnson family are now contesting this unequal division of family property, which leaves landless eight of the fifteen Rocky Gap households descended from Bob Johnson (see Figures 2 and 6). They argue that since the land passed to "the heirs of Bob Johnson," they—his descendants and heirs—should all have equal rights in the estate. In accordance with the logic of this argument, one couple who legally own only 10.8 acres are claiming, as heirs of Bob Johnson, to own 57 acres (jointly with others, but this is not always made explicit). Many other land owners, however, view this argument not as a way of increasing their holdings but rather as an assault on their property rights, and much of the Johnson family is consequently beset with dispute and rancor.

It perhaps was a desire to circumvent such family conflict over the proper distribution of family land that led Noah Bradley, son of Abraham Bradley, to compose a rather unusual will. Most residents do not write wills, either selling or giving their property in their lifetimes to their children or others or allowing it to pass automatically to their heirs upon their death. When Noah Bradley died in 1940, however, he left a will providing that his property was to pass after his wife's death to his eleven children "to share and share alike as long as they live a life estate in the said property." Further, with the death of each heir "the interest of the party shall go to the remainder of the living survivors" with the last surviving child becoming the sole beneficiary. As an effort to realize the concept of family property, this will has met with equivocal results. Today most of Noah Bradley's land, while it is jointly owned by his surviving children as stipulated, lies fallow and uninhabited. For although one son and daughter-in-law live in "the home place," the house that Noah Bradley built many years ago, none of his other five surviving children will build homes and live on any portion of this estate because each knows that should he or she predecease the others, his

or her spouse and children will legally lose their homes. So
although Noah Bradley's will has forestalled the unequal sub-
division and possible sale of his estate and the disputes that
sometimes accompany or follow this process, his property has
not exactly been shared among his children in the way he
probably intended. Indeed, his children express resentment
over the terms of this will, which as they often point out
effectively disinherit most of his grandchildren.

As these two cases illustrate, family rights and individual
rights to land are by no means always in harmony. For although most land owners most of the time have chosen to
pass their land on to their children or sell it to other family
members, the specific ways in which they have done this and
the eventual outcomes of their actions have not always met
with the approval of other family members, who consider
themselves also to have family rights to the land in question.

The Coincidence of Family and Community Memberships

Although the family land of the top of the mountain is said
to have always been passed on in the family, the timing, manner, and direction of its passage have clearly been neither au-
tomatic nor inevitable. For just as community residence is
explained in terms both of longstanding family roots in particular areas and shifting individual choices, so too land ownership patterns, although they are said to result from the fact
that the land of each community is "family land" that has
always been in the family, are also understood to result from
the various rightful or legitimate decisions and acts of individual owners.

As seen, owners' actions in disposing of their property may
lead to recurring perceived inequities in the distribution of
family land. More than this, and more problematically, they

may also result in its progressive alienation. For although land is usually passed on in the family, albeit often in a very circuitous fashion, some land owners have not given or sold their land to either their descendants or other close kin.

Some, as noted, have sold out to land companies, with the result that the top of the mountain today comprises only a few hundred acres of resident owned land surrounded on all sides by many thousands of acres of company land.[2] To be sure, most of the land that was sold to these companies is located on the relatively marginal and inaccessible steep hillsides, and most of the land in the more desirable flats has been retained by residents (with the major exception of Mine Flats). Even in these areas, however, land appears to have been often and for long sold outside the family. For example, we have previously seen that in 1896 Robert Johnson, founder of the Johnson family of Rocky Gap, "sold off" 61.2 acres to a son of Abraham Bradley. To give a more recent example, in the 1960s Bill Green, one of the Campbells, purchased 6.5 acres in Campbell Flats from Bobby Johnson, a great-grandson of Robert Johnson. How Bobby Johnson, who is now deceased, had originally come to acquire this property could not be determined. These examples are by no means isolated cases. Of the 404.3 acres of privately owned land on the mountain, at least 161.2 acres have been transferred apparently across family lines one or more times. Indeed, the figure is probably somewhat higher, for detailed ownership histories could not be reconstructed for all tracts.

Despite these sales to non-family members, however, current residence and land ownership patterns are spoken of as the outcome of a long history of passing land on in the family; and this is seemingly confirmed by the fact that most of the residents and land owners of each of the mountain's com-

---

[2]But most of this land-company hegemony in the neighborhood and throughout the mountains of Baker County was achieved through buying out the nonresident holders of large land grants.

munities are members of the family associated with that community, the descendants and affines of the descendants of the
community settler. Family members are not widely scattered
among several communities as they might be expected to be
as a result of land sales across family lines. How is this circumstance to be understood?

Without doubt, much of the present coincidence of family
and community boundaries is explained by people's predilections for passing their land on to their children or to other
close kin, as illustrated in the cases of the tracts once owned
by Ned Bradley, Bob Johnson, and Noah Bradley. On the
other hand, however, there is evidence to suggest that land
ownership and residence may also sometimes be important
influencing factors in the conceptual delineation of family
groups.

As seen in the preceding chapter, the family groups of the
top of the mountain are not, strictly speaking, genealogical
groups. They are rather, fluid and slowly shifting social
groupings, the composition of which depends not only on
genealogical givens but also on the perception and formulation
of existing and changing social relationships; and family members are those kin who are both genealogically and socially
and psychologically close. Land may be an important medium
for the expression and, to an extent, the creation of these close
family bonds, individuals expressing their affinity for a particular family by seeking to own land and live in a community
and, by the same token, family members exhibiting their close
ties to them in making land and homes available.

Further details pertaining to Marj and Cal Jones' sale of
twenty-six acres to Cal's brother and sister-in-law, Alice and
Eli Jones, are illustrative of this process. As seen in Figure 3,
the mother of Cal and Eli Jones was Sadie Bradley Jones, the
daughter of Abraham Bradley's brother's son. Sadie's parents
lived in the community of Sourwood Grove at the southeastern foot of the mountain, and Sadie continued to live there
after her marriage to Cal and Eli's father, Zachary Jones. Cal

married one of the great-granddaughters of Abraham Bradley and moved to Bradley Flats, where he and his wife eventually acquired twenty-six acres from her father Ned Bradley as related earlier. Later they sold this property to Cal's brother and sister-in-law, Eli and Alice Jones, and they too moved to Bradley Flats. When Marj and Cal Jones sold their land to this couple they were clearly selling to their close kin. And Alice and Eli are members in good standing of the Bradley family group; they are socially close to other family members, and one son has married a daughter of Lucy and Pete Dalton and resides in Bradley Flats on a lot this latter couple has given him and his wife.

It is possible, however, that Alice and Eli's status as family members may not always have been so clear and unambiguous. This is suggested by the rather indeterminate family membership of a third brother, Bill Jones. Bill is married to Dorothy Bradley Jones, the great-granddaughter of Abraham Bradley and granddaughter of Hiram Johnson. Their multiple genealogical links to both the Bradley family and the Johnson family of Mine Flats are illustrated in Figure 8. Dorothy Bradley Jones grew up in Mine Flats, but Bill has never resided on the mountain, and the couple has made their home in Sourwood Grove since their marriage. Although they regularly attend church in Bradley Flats and occasionally visit kin in Bradley Flats and Mine Flats, they do not often see other neighborhood residents. Many (but not all) members of the Bradley family and the Johnson family of Mine Flats include Bill and Dorothy Jones in their personal kindreds and sometimes refer to them as either "Bradleys" or "Johnsons." Most residents, however, forced to rely mainly on an assessment of their multiple genealogical links, are uncertain of how best to evaluate their family status. More often, the issue does not arise: I think residents simply do not often consider Bill and Dorothy Jones and other non-residents when they speak of the mountain's families.

It seems very possible, however, that should Bill and Dor-

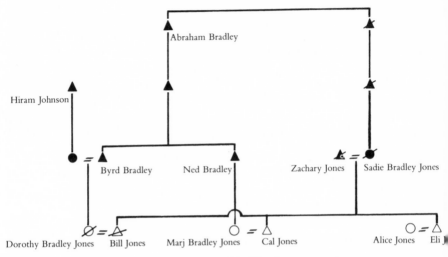

Figure 8. The Joneses.

othy Jones have the opportunity and choose to select among
and act on their kin relationships by moving to the mountain,
their family membership would in time become clear and unambiguous to all. This, I suggest, is precisely what occurred
earlier in the case of Eli and Alice Jones, whose clear inclusion
as members of the Bradley family is probably based as much
on their long-term residence and land ownership in Bradley
Flats and their daily close association with other members of
the Bradley family as on their multiple affinal and consanguineal links to them. This is not to suggest that family membership is conferred by residence in a community nor lost by
non-residence. As Figure 6 illustrates, everyone who lives in
a community is not automatically considered to be a member
of the family associated with that community, and conversely,
everyone considered to be a family member does not necessarily live on family land, in the community settled by the
family's founding ancestor. Nonetheless, it is probable that
residence and land ownership play significant roles in the resolution of genealogical ambiguity. Families and communities
may thus come to coincide not only, as seen, because residents

of the mountain usually sell their land and reside near to their close kin, but also because in many cases this may be one of the reasons they think of themselves as close.

A Historical Perspective

According to people on the top of the mountain, members of a family tend to live together in the same community and retain their land among themselves because they all have ancestral rights to the land. These rights are said to derive from the circumstances of early settlement, each community comprising the land settled by a family's founding ancestor plus additional acreages acquired by his descendants over the years, all of which has been passed on to his descendants and heirs.

As seen, each community is today inhabited primarily by members of the family said to be descended from the community's early settler because, as residents see it, family land has always been passed on in the family and also probably because residence and land ownership patterns influence conceptions of family configurations. More than this, however, families and communities may come to coincide also through the redelineation of communities in accordance with the changing locations of families.

Consider, for example, the implications of Robert Bradley's earlier mentioned purchase in 1896 of 61.2 acres from Robert Johnson. Although this tract, which is located just north of the county highway, originally belonged to Robert Johnson, the founder of the Johnson family of Rocky Gap, it is now considered to be Bradley family land and part of Bradley Flats. Residents who know of this sale nonetheless maintain that Rocky Gap and Bradley Flats are each situated on the lands settled respectively by Robert Johnson and Abraham Bradley. They explain that the tract Robert Johnson sold to Robert Bradley constitutes part of the additional acreages purchased by Abraham Bradley's descendants and was but a temporary and unimportant acquisition for Robert Johnson, for the land that he actually settled and later passed on to his descendants was obviously located further south, in the community of Rocky Gap.

Since present notions of the configurations of family groups have probably not prevailed throughout the mountain's history, it is of course very possible that at the time of this sale Robert Johnson and Robert Bradley were not considered to be members of separate families and that Robert Johnson was therefore not really "selling off" his land. But the logic of residents' explanations of why some of what was once Robert Johnson's land is now Bradley family land also suggests that neither families *nor* communities may be as enduring and immutable as is commonly supposed.

An analysis of a relationship between kinship groups and residence groups that is in some respects similar to this is found in a recent paper by Renato Rosaldo. In "Where Precision Lies: 'The hill people once lived on a hill,' " Rosaldo explores the historical connections between apparently differing kinds of social groupings among the Ilongot of the Philippines. Finding that a single Ilongot category word (*be:rtan*) is used to designate groups that vary from local groups at one extreme to nonlocalized and overlapping nonunilineal descent groups at the other, he remarks: "The problem is as vexing as it is familiar: the social unit appears to vacillate between Maine's opposition of kinship and territory—or, as we would say today, descent groups and local groups."[3]

In addressing this problem, Rosaldo follows "the lead provided by the native model," which explains all *be:rtan*, regardless of their present characteristics, in terms of primal coresidence—for example, "the hill people once lived on a hill." He adduces historical evidence indicating that the radically

[3]In *The Interpretation of Symbolism*, ed. Roy Willis, ASA Studies 3 (New York: John Wiley, 1975), 4.

different types of social units the Ilongot group together as
be:rtan may represent but "differing phases in a single historical process."[4] Ilongot local groups and descent groups are
thus found indeed to be the same kind of social grouping, and
the Ilongot designation of both as *be:rtan* is seen to reflect the
diachronic processes underlying the synchronic data of social
organization.

Like the Ilongot, people of the top of the mountain explain
their residence groups in terms of early co-residence. But
mountain residents' conceptions of the history of their communities, unlike Ilongot categories, may well owe more to
the present than to the past. This is lent considerable credence
by the fact that people usually do not know with certainty the
exact locations of the tracts said to have been settled by their
nineteenth-century forebears. This is true even in the one case
where the original deed has been preserved: the document
recording the purchase of Abraham Bradley's two hundred
acres describes this property as bounded on the northeast by
"too poplars and a hickry," on the northwest by "a shugar-
tree," on the west by "a chesnut," on the south by "a hickry,"
"a pine," and "a stake and hickry," and on the southeast by
"a chesnut."

Despite uncertainties about the precise locations of the property of their forebears, people on the mountain surmise that
these tracts must have been located in the present communities
of Campbell Flats, Rocky Gap, Bradley Flats, and Mine Flats
and subsequently passed on in the family because these communities are today inhabited primarily or exclusively by the
descendants and heirs of Isaiah Foley Campbell, Robert Johnson, Abraham Bradley, and Hiram Johnson. In view of this
logic, might not the indigenous notion that each community
is composed of "what you might call family land" that has
always been "passed on in the family" be best interpreted less
as a literal description of what was than as a symbolic repre-

[4]Ibid., 17-18.

sentation of what is? From this perspective a community becomes the place where a family lives, and a family becomes,
to a large extent, a group of kinfolk who live together. Communities may then not be geographical givens any more than
families are genealogical givens, and the contours of both are
seen to evolve and change together in accordance with shifting
residence patterns and social relationships.

Families and Communities

It should not be concluded from the above discussion that
families are "really" local groups disguised by an idiom of
kinship or that communities are actually localized kinship
groups. For to reduce (and thereby dismiss) one to the other
is to ignore a fundamental point, namely that "communities"
and "families" are conceptually distinct. Just as Rosaldo finds
among the Ilongot that residential and descent groups are
really but different phases in the developmental cycle of a
single kind of social unit, so too it is seen that in general
outline the families and communities of the top of the mountain are actually one when viewed through a historical lens.
But the Ilongot use one category word *(be:rtan)* to refer to a
number of apparently different kinds of social groups. In contrast, residents of the top of the mountain speak of what is
by, and large, from a long-term perspective, a single social
grouping in terms of apparently radically opposed principles
of group formation.

Although family and community membership configurations tend to coincide and residents trace the origin of each to
the arrival on the mountain of the same four men, communities and families are discussed in terms that suggest they are
quite different. Families are said to be composed primarily of
people who share blood that has been naturally inherited from
a common ancestor. Communities, on the other hand, are

said to be composed of the people who reside in a particular area both because they have family rights to the land of the community and because they have elected to reside there. This contrast between communities and families has analogies in mountain residents' ideas pertaining to marriage. When speaking of spouses and affines as family members, people tend to stress the notion that "like marries like," that spouses are naturally attracted to one another because of their natural similarities. But mountain residents, like other Americans, also think that marriage is not something that just happens—it is also chosen or willed by the individuals concerned. Thus, while the relationship between spouses is on the one hand compelled by their inner natures, it is also voluntary.[5]

These two components—natural ascription and free choice— are distinguished in residents' statements pertaining to families and communities. When speaking of a group of people as a family, residents emphasize the "natural" bonds among family members, an idea that is often symbolically expressed through the concept of shared "flesh and blood" inherited from a common ancestor. When speaking of what is often the same group of people as a community, however, they talk not of blood but of family land. Like blood, the family land of each community is said to be inherited from a common ancestor and shared by family members, who "all got rights to it" by virtue of their descent from this ancestor. But unlike the shared blood that unites family members, family land is not automatically or naturally inherited. Rather, it is "passed on" from one family member to another through the conscious and willful acts of individual residents and land owners. Thus, while people are born into or at least (as affines) born to families, they choose their communities and their neighbors.

---

[5]A similar and more comprehensive discussion of Western concepts regarding conjugal love and marriage, based on interviews with Jamaican informants, is presented in Jack Alexander, "The Cultural Domain of Marriage," *American Ethnologist* 5 (Feb. 1978), 5–14.

As members of the same family, people "stick together through thick and thin" because it is in their nature to do so. Considered as community members, however, they reside near to one another and "stick together" because they have elected to do so. "Families" and "communities" at base then represent not different groupings, but rather different principles of social organization and relationship. While these principles are diametrically opposed, they are also complementary. For the fact that kinfolk, as neighbors and members of a community, freely decide to live near one another and share their land serves to prove just how natural their family relationships truly are.

CHURCHES

History

Residents of the top of the mountain are uncertain of the religious backgrounds and persuasions of their nineteenth-century forebears. They do know, however, that at least subsequent to their ancestors' settlement on the mountain, all those who attended religious services at all went to the nearest church, Sourwood Grove Baptist Church, located in the small community at the foot of the mountain where both Robert Johnson and Abraham Bradley had formerly resided.

In 1909 some of these mountain residents requested and recevied permission from the "mother church" in Sourwood Grove to organize their own church on the mountain. The business minutes of what is now known as the Cherokee Bluff Missionary Baptist Church record its first official gathering as follows:

> August 5, 1909. A presbytery being called for the purpose of organizing a new Church at _____, Tennessee and after electing _____ moderator and _____ clerk and receiving 27 members by letter and after reading the articles of faith and the

administration of the Church covenant the Church was pronounced an independent body.

The new congregation had no church building, and monthly services were held at first in members' homes and later in a one-room schoolhouse in Bradley Flats. But the church grew over the years, and in 1929 the congregation was able to build a one-room "church house" next to the cemetery in Bradley Flats. Later, in 1950, they added two new Sunday School classrooms to the church house, which was by then being used for bi-weekly services.

Church minutes and membership lists indicate that throughout the period 1909-50, most of those mountain residents who are now thought to be or to have been members of the Johnson family of Rocky Gap, the Bradley family, and the Johnson family of Mine Flats belonged to or attended the Cherokee Bluff Missionary Baptist Church. (Most of the Campbells continued to belong to the Sourwood Grove Baptist Church, which they point out is only a short vertical drop away from Campbell Flats and was therefore more convenient for them to attend in the days before the advent of the automobile and before the paving of the local roads.) In the ensuing years, however, most of the Johnsons of Rocky Gap and of Mine Flats eventually left the Cherokee Bluff Missionary Baptist Church.

In the case of the Johnsons of Mine Flats, the break was gradual and generally unremarked upon. It appears that many of the members of this family who had once regularly attended this church began to "backslide"—they slowly lost interest in and eventually ceased to attend services, and many of their children later failed to join the church at all. By 1976, although several members of the Johnson family of Mine Flats were still listed on the membership rolls, none took an active part in church affairs nor attended services more than occasionally.

The departure of the Johnsons of Rocky Gap, on the other hand, was relatively sudden and dramatic and was attended by considerable acrimony. The bitterness that accompanied this split is reflected in the church minutes of the period. The minutes for April 1953, for example, state that

> The Sourwood Grove Baptist Church wrote for letters of Sister _____, _____, _____, and _____ [four women of the Johnson family of Rocky Gap]. The Church voted for the deacon to talk to the deacon of Sourwood Grove Church why the Church cannot give them a letter. Also a letter to be read in there Church that in there standing the Church cannot recommend them in good standing.

According to residents, in the early 1950s members of the Johnson family of Rocky Gap and the Bradley family fell into dispute over some now forgotten issue or issues. The Johnsons soon ceased to attend the Cherokee Bluff Missionary Baptist Church, claiming that the Bradleys "ran" the church, and decided to establish their own independent congregation. The mother church of Cherokee Bluff refused to sanction this undertaking, however, so the Johnsons "went down the mountain" and joined the Sourwood Grove Baptist Church, where they then sought and received permission to organize a new congregation—the Rocky Gap Baptist Church—in 1954.

Churches and Families

As a result of the split between the Johnsons of Rocky Gap and the Bradleys, the top of the mountain, although having a population of only 198 individuals, now boasts two churches, both of the Southern Baptist denominations (as are, in fact, all but two—one Methodist and one Holiness Church—of the twenty-two churches of the mountainous northwestern section of Baker County). But despite this proliferation of churches, residents of the mountain are not, as a group, notably church-oriented. Certainly, many are faithful church members who attend, as the saying goes, "whenever the church house doors are open." But many others, although they are usually formal church members—that is, they have been baptized and are listed on the membership rolls of a church— attend seldom or at best sporadically. Consequently a typical Sunday morning service at either of the mountain's two churches is attended by only twenty to forty individuals. Evidently, then, the presence of two churches on the mountain has very little to do with problems of overcrowding.

This phenomenon—large numbers of churches with very small active memberships—has been remarked upon for the Appalachian region in general;[1] and Weller has ascribed it to the people's "religious individualism," or a seemingly selfish inability to cooperate and get along with one another:

> This individualism rejects all forms of discipline in religion. If a church does not suit the mountaineer by preaching what he wants to hear in the way he wants to hear it or does not give him enough opportunity to assert himself and be heard, he will quit and go somewhere else. If he is a strong personality, he may even form his own church, where he is the minister and "boss," perhaps erecting a building in his front yard and naming the church after his family. . . . The mountains hold a great many of these "churches," based on the personal desires and feelings of their members, usually split off from a larger group—ingrown little bodies that pamper their people in order to keep them coming and thus confirm them in their favorite prejudices. Up many hollows, churches stand side by side or across the road from each other, seemingly glaring at each other.[2]

Applied to the top of the mountain, Weller's "explanation" leaves much to be desired, for the presence of two churches in this neighborhood appears to have less to do with religious "individualism," however defined, than with a strong tendency for each family to act as a group and independently of

[1]See, for example, Earl D.C. Brewer, "Religion and the Churches," in *The Southern Appalachian Region*, ed. Ford.
[2]*Yesterday's People*, 125-26.

the others in religious affairs. As seen, most of the Cambells belong to the Sourwood Grove Baptist Church, the Johnsons of Rocky Gap to the Rocky Gap Baptist Church, the Bradleys to the Cherokee Bluff Missionary Baptist Church, and most of the Johnsons of Mine Flats to no church at all. This pattern is reflected in many residents' comments on their churches, for they frequently associate each with a particular family. Thus, for example: "When the Johnsons formed their church . . ." and "The Bradleys, in their church. . . ."

That there is indeed a close relationship between churches and families is demonstrated with greater clarity at the neighborhood's annual "homecomings." Although all four family groups of the top of the mountain do not have their own church, each does have its own family or community cemetery, where the founder of the family is buried and where many of his descendants continue to be buried to this day. Every year each of these cemeteries becomes the site and the religious focus of an event known on the mountain as a homecoming and reportedly referred to in other parts of Appalachia variously as a "graveyard reunion," "decoration," "May Meeting," or "October Meeting."[3] Since the homecoming will be discussed at some length later in this chapter, it will not be explored in detail here. Suffice it to say at this point that on these occasions the family is seemingly treated as a distinct spiritual and religious group. Although "everyone" is invited to these events and they often attract large crowds, they are also family events that explicitly focus on and celebrate the idea of the spiritual unity of all family members, both living and dead, and their eventual heavenly reunion. Moreover, the homecoming celebrations of the Johnsons of

[3]Elizabeth R. Hooker, *Religion in the Highlands: Native Churches and Missionary Enterprises in the Southern Appalachian Area* (New York: Home Mission Council, 1933), 125-28; Gwen Neville Kennedy, "Kinfolks and the Covenant: Ethnic Community Among Southern Presbyterians," in *The New Ethnicity: Perspectives from Ethnology*, ed. John W. Bennett (Proceedings of the American Ethnological Society, 1973), 265-68.

Rocky Gap and the Bradleys, both of whom have their own formally organized churches, are spoken of as though each were hosted by a family/church. That is, they are interchangeably called "family" homecomings and "church" homecomings, and it is perfectly proper to say of the same event that "The Bradleys are having a homecoming" and "The Cherokee Bluff Church is having a homecoming."

It thus appears that choice of church membership (or nonmembership in the case of most of the Johnsons of Mine Flats) is an important corollary of family membership, the spiritual unity of church members and of homecoming participants reflecting and reinforcing the "natural" unity of the family.

The Family of Christ

From the above, it appears that the social organization of the top of the mountain is replicated on the religious plane, the church serving, at least in part, to sanctify and lend legitimacy to the family/community. But while it is no doubt true that the churches of the neighborhood derive from and affirm the social order, residents' ideas regarding the relationship of the church to the earthly world of men and women are anything but Durkheimian.[4] Mountain residents disavow any connection between profane social groups of any sort and the spiritual "family of Christ," which is the Church.

The family of Christ or the Church is thought to be composed not of those who live in a particular place or are descended from a particular individual, but rather of those who have been "saved" or "reborn" through their personal acceptance of Christ's offer of salvation, an offer that is made to

---

[4]Emile Durkheim's theory stressing an isomorphic relationship between religious organization and belief and social organization is expounded in his classic work, *The Elementary Forms of the Religious Life*, trans. Joseph Ward Swain (1915; rpt. New York: Free Press, 1965).

each and every individual regardless of his or her personal and social attributes. "God," residents say, "is no respecter of persons," and the church is "open to everyone who accepts Christ." Although all the members of both churches of the top of the mountain are related to one another, this fact is generally ignored in the religious context. A person is not thought to belong to a particular church because other members of his family or community belong, but because Christ, through that church, "reached out" to him as an individual. What unites church members is not that they are kin but that they are "brothers and sisters in Christ." Salvation and church membership is thus neither a state to which one is born nor a state that the individual achieves through the exercise of personal gifts or prerogatives. It comes about rather through the individual's acceptance of a universal invitation: "Christ is knocking—will you answer?"

This invitation, while universal, is also highly personal. As Bruce has noted of the "camp-meeting" religious beliefs of the antebellum South: "It was not just that there was a general offer of grace which one could accept or reject, but rather that the Lord had made the offer to each individual as an individual."[5] The belief in an intimate relationship between the individual and the Divine is reflected and expressed in many of the hymns that are popular on the top of the mountain:

> There are days I'd like to be
> All alone with Christ, my Lord,
> I can tell Him of my troubles
> All alone, all alone.
>
> Do you know Him, know my Savior,
> Do you know His wondrous love
> And mighty power?
> You would make my Savior yours
> This very hour,
> If you knew Him,

[5] *And They All Sang Hallelujah*, 111.

As I know Him,
You would make my Savior yours
This very hour.

As these verses suggest, while Christ's invitation is believed
to be extended to everyone, people also stress the personalistic
aspects of salvation. On the mountain Christ is spoken of as
a "personal Savior," and those individuals who are part of the
family of Christ by virtue of their salvation or rebirth are each
thought to enjoy an intimate friendship with Jesus.

Church Organization

Both churches of the top of the mountain belong to the
Baker County Southern Baptist Association. Their membership, however, does not imply submission to any governing
body or principle, for the association explictly disavows any
authority over its member churches. In 1976, for example,
two of the small churches of the mountainous section of the
county angrily withdrew from the association following its
refusal to take any action against one of the "Valley" member
churches which had recently ordained several female deacons.
These two mountain churches maintained—and most residents of the top of the mountain agreed with them—that the
ordination of female deacons "goes against the Bible." In de-
fense of their position they cited I Timothy 3:12: "Let the deacons be the husbands of one wife, ruling their children and
their own houses well." The president of the county association, however, issued a statement pointing out that each congregation is an independent body and that the association
therefore has no power to dictate to its member churches.
Residents of the top of the mountain were in full agreement
with this, although they had very little sympathy with the
innovations introduced by the Valley church in question. Each
congregation, they argue, has unmediated access to the word

of God, and if they should choose to ignore God's will such matters cannot be legislated by denominational decree.

Mountain residents' beliefs regarding the religious signifi-cance of the intimate relationship between individuals and their personal Savior admit very little in the way of centralized church authority and formal leadership. Every member of the congregation is thought to be in direct communion with the Holy, and no one person or group is considered to have priv-ileged spiritual access. Within the church, formal leadership roles are minimal and are constantly muted. Although both churches of the mountain have an elected deacon body, the role of the deacons is very ambiguous. For while they are charged with providing moral leadership and guidance, the deacons are loathe to appear to exert any influence over the congregation and in fact make a point of bringing all issues and concerns, however minor, before the entire church mem-bership in a totally nonpartisan manner. This is not to say, of course, that their views on any and all matters are not well-known to the congregation and vice versa. Nor is it to deny that residents recognize that some individuals are more force-ful and influential than others. Influence and leadership, how-ever, is not to be identified with formal leadership roles. It is, rather, a personal gift or talent, which is not restricted to deacons or even to males and which should always be exer-cised subtly and informally. For the deacons to assert their authority as deacons would undoubtedly be considered to be an anathema, suggestive of the possibility that a humanly de-vised hierarchy could be interposed between the individual and the Divine.

In both churches of the top of the mountain, church busi-ness is formally conducted in monthly business meetings fol-lowing the Sunday evening service. These meetings are "moderated" either by the pastor or by one of the deacons. All issues and proposals are voted on by a show of hands. The vote is almost always unanimous, and several church members noted that generally no issue is formally raised in these meetings unless it has already been discussed informally and a tentative consensus reached. The focus appears to be less on the efficient conduct of business than on maintaining and exhibiting the solidarity of the church.

As is true of the deacons, the pastor or preacher is not set apart from or above the other members of the congregation. Many people are given a chance to play leading roles in the service, the pastor in one of the pews sitting quietly with the others. When the time comes for him to deliver his message, or sermon, he is modest and reticent, like the preacher at a mountain funeral described by Elizabeth Hooker: "In low, uncertain tones he expresses his dread of preventing someone else from speaking, 'Yet,' he goes on, 'we are commanded to come before the people in the presence of God and trust He will take possession of our minds and cause us to speak.' "[6]

Neither pastor of the two churches of the top of the mountain has received any formal seminary training, both having been ordained shortly after receiving a "call to preach."[7] But lack of formal training is not considered to be a detriment. What Bruce has noted of early Baptist views regarding the ministry is still true on the mountain: "Conversion, a direct experience in salvation, believed to be initiated by the Lord, was the crucial qualification for the ministry, as it was for church membership. Such a direct experience of God's power was felt to be far superior to any enlightenment that might be gained from a wordly education."[8] Many residents of the mountain express the view that some seminary training for ministers "probably don't hurt none." But most are also of the opinion that "too much" formal education can be detri-

---

[6]*Religion in the Highlands*, 69-70.

[7]Neither of these men are neighborhood residents, although both are from nearby mountain communities. This phenomenon is quite common, for most of the ministers of the mountain churches of Baker County are not residents of the communities in which their churches are located. I unfortunately did not think to inquire into the matter, however, and am therefore unable to comment on the possible significance of the pattern.

[8]*And They All Sang Hallelujah*, 38.

mental, often making preachers too "bossy" and "know-it-all." A "good" preacher is one who, among other things, is humble in the face of the Lord's power, acknowledging always that he is but a frail mortal like everyone else and that his message is the work of the Lord.

Religious Services

Beliefs regarding the universality and individuality of religious experience are reflected not only in the muting of formal leadership roles at both the denominational and congregational levels, but also in the dominant style and mood of church services. The formal ritual and liturgies that elsewhere often mediate the relationship between the individual and the Divine are almost entirely absent on the top of the mountain. Instead, religious services are marked by an informality and spontaneity that both derives from and encourages active individual participation. All members of the congregation are believed to be, at least potentially, in direct communion with the Lord, and the religious experience of the individual is both the basis and the focus of the church service. Its primary goal is that of realizing this potential as fully as possible or, as Pearsall has observed in another East Tennessee neighborhood, to "stir souls to repentance and to the achievement of a positive and intimate relation with God."[9]

Something of this religious style is conveyed by the following composite description of a typical worship service based on tape recordings of twelve mountain services.

Church services on the mountain invariably begin with congregational singing, usually initiated by the "choir leader" or "singing leader." Although it may sometimes be necessary for him (in my experience, always a man) to personally select

[9]*Little Smoky Ridge*, 107.

many of the hymns, he tries to ensure that all members of the congregation, both young and old, have ample opportunity to request their own personal favorites and often coaxes others to come forward to help lead the singing. Throughout, participation, rather than musical skills or reverential propriety, is emphasized. Matthews' description of church singings in Middle Tennessee might well have been written of the top of the mountain:

> Well-trained voices are not held in high esteem. . . . The emphasis is placed on willingness to sing. At some time during every singing someone is likely to remind the group that "we are singing with the spirit as well as with the understanding".
> . . . Individuality and creativity in manner of playing and singing . . . are highly desirable . . . singers seem to enjoy abandonment, entirely free of inhibitions or emotional restraints.
> . . . The announcer for the convention or the leader of the singing school makes sure that everyone who will lead a song or take part in a special number does so. The best . . . leader is the one who gets everyone of every age to take his turn in directing the singing.[10]

As a result of the choir leader's endeavors to ensure that no one is left out, church "singings" on the top of the mountain are often quite protracted. The president of the county's Southern Baptist Association noted that while the Valley churches usually have one "special" (a hymn requested by a member of the congregation or sung by a small group), the mountain churches will take requests indefinitely because this provides an opportunity to involve everyone in the service. Yet while all members of the congregation are indeed encouraged to express themselves and to take an active role in this as in all other parts of the service, no one individual or group should "show off" or seek to dominate. Accordingly, no one ever requests or leads more than one or two hymns,

[10]*Neighbor and Kin*, 83–84.

and singings are therefore not of indefinite duration, most lasting no more than half an hour.

When it is evident that there are no further requests, the choir leader may make a jocular remark about "turning the preacher loose," and the pastor, who has been sitting with the congregation until this time, comes forward to "open the service." He first welcomes the congregation:

> . . . we're thankful for each one that has come, and we want to welcome you here . . . and we just want you to feel free and just obey the call of the Spirit. And you've heard it said many times that as long as you follow the call of the Spirit, then you will never be—uh—out of order. So let's be obedient today. . . . So again, we welcome you. (9-12-76)

Following his welcoming remarks, the pastor invites the congregation to come forward to the altar:

> Let's come together. You know, I was just thinking how you see people, you know, some here, some there. You know, sometimes them things get scattered out, and you see one here and one over there. . . . You know the problem, you know, one's over here and you can go over there and get him. . . . But boys, when you get in the middle of it, something's gonna take place here now. So that's the way it is tonight. . . . Come up here! Let's get closer together like we love one another. Come on up here! Let's get in the altar together. . . . Maybe you're not able to kneel, but we would forive you, but we would ask you to come in the front seat if you're not able to kneel. Come in the front seat. Come as close as you can. Come on, boys, just as close as we can here tonight. We—we're brothers and sisters in Christ, and it don't matter if we kneel down here and get on somebody's toes. That's all right, it don't hurt none, boys, the hurt will soon be over. Come on, let's get closer together! (8-21-76)

When all are gathered in the front of the church, they join together in singing one of several familiar hymns that everyone seems to know by heart. As they sing, the preacher and the members of the congregation, many of them in tears on occasion, walk about and greet each other personally with a handshake or an embrace. When the hymn is over and everyone has "extended the right hand of Christian fellowship" to everyone else, the pastor invites the congregation to join together in prayer. Some of the men kneel down on the floor, but most people remain standing in the area directly in front of the altar or take seats in the first few pews. Each person prays individually, many in a soft undertone but most silently with heads bowed. When the last voice has died away, the preacher offers a few concluding words of prayer aloud, and all return to their seats.

At this point in the service a collection may be taken up, after which the pastor invites various soloists and groups of singers to come forward. First come the members of each Sunday School class, beginning with the youngest, children aged about three to six, and ending with the "young adults," aged about eighteen to forty-five. Each class sings one or two hymns they have rehearsed previously in their classes or in the homes of classmates. The pastor then asks if anyone else has a song. After considerable coaxing, various individuals and small groups of singers known for their "good singing" may present their renditions of one or two currently popular gospel and inspirational songs, such as "Hallelujah Morning," "There's Nothing That My God Can't Do," and "I Won't Have to Worry Anymore."

After everyone who is willing has had a chance to sing, the preacher stands and begins his message. The general topic and the Biblical passages to be cited have usually been selected in advance, but the text is unprepared, the pastors of the top of the mountain preferring to rely on divine inspiration:

> Boys, He will give us a message—uh—that's pleasing to Him, that suits Him. We're just an old mouthpiece, and we just thank God for that. . . . Now boys, I tell you, we just can't do a thing up here, old Jim just can't do a thing, you know. God called us to preach, and all that we can do is—uh—be the

old mouthpiece—uh, uh—if anything is accomplished. So that's all we want to do today, and we need your prayers, and just pray that God will get old Jim out of the way and, you know, that He will take control here and use the old mouthpiece. (8-29-76)

Following the reading of a Biblical passage, the pastor begins to expound on its meaning and relevance for modern times. As he proceeds he often, but not always, begins to "get the Spirit" and launches into a style of delivery that has been described by several observers of mountain religious services in Appalachia.[11] In this style he becomes excited, his voice rising and falling as it alternates between a shout and whisper, and he paces rapidly back and forth in front of the altar delivering his message in short phrases, each separated by an "uh!" and a quick intake of breath:

> You know, we heard this story
>   about this old boy—uh
> that killed just a great big
>   giant one time—uh
> with just a little stone
>   there—uh
> a little pebble—uh!
> We heard how—uh
> how David throwed the stone—uh
> and God done the rest!
> Now boys—uh
> a lot of times if we would just
>   make a little effort—uh, uh
> then God'll pave the way—uh!
> So this old boy—uh
> all he done—uh, uh
> was throw the stone—uh
> and God done the rest—uh!
> God is looking down today—uh, uh!

[11]See, for example, Hooker, *Religion in the Highlands*, 68-70; Pearsall, *Little Smoky Ridge*, 111-13.

> He loves us just as much—uh
> as He loved old John the Baptist—uh
> that forerunner yonder—uh
> of Jesus Christ—uh!
> The one the Bible said—uh
> was His forerunner—uh
> the one we might say—uh
> that kinda paved the way—uh, uh
> for this One—uh
> that they were singing about—uh
> the greatest name that I know—uh!
> And boys, that is true today—uh!
> The greatest name—uh
> that we can say today—uh
> is *Jesus*—uh! (8-29-76)

Most messages, like this excerpt, focus on and interweave the themes of Christ's love; the necessity for human obedience, acceptance, "a little effort," repentance; and the blessings that will flow from this—God will "take control," "pave the way," bring untold joys. One or more times the preacher invites sinners and backsliders to come forward and be saved or renew their faith, exhorting them with shouts of the joys awaiting the faithful in heaven. After a period lasting, in my experience, anywhere from fifteen to sixty minutes, depending on the "will of the Spirit," the preacher begins to regain control of himself. As he assumes his normal tone and style of speech, he starts to draw the service to a close by asking if "anyone else has a message or a testimony":

Maybe tonight you have something just on your heart. Maybe just a testimony or a prayer or maybe you would just like to obey the Holy will of God—whatever. We don't want to rush the service. We just want to do this by the Holy Spirit's name. Now we want to give you the opportunity—just whatever it might be, whatever's on your heart—like I say, just obey the Holy Spirit. Anyone got a word or a prayer? (9-1-76)

At this time a few individuals may stand and speak briefly and in very general terms of the joys of being a Christian or the importance of trusting in God. When it is apparent that no one has anything further to add, the preacher suggests that they close the service and calls on one of the men of the congregation to lead everyone in prayer. This prayer marks the end of the service.

Different kinds of religious services—Sunday morning worship services, Wednesday night prayer meetings, revivals, funerals, homecomings—differ from one another in the ordering and the amount of emphasis placed on the various components of the service. But all are similar to the composite service above in exhibiting the same general style of religious observance. This style is one that stresses and draws upon the freedom and spontaneous emotion of the individual. Rigid formalism, anything that might restrict or restrain individual expression is rejected, and each member of the congregation is encouraged to say or do "whatever's on your heart."

Interpretations

Fastening upon certain of the beliefs and assumptions that are either explicit or implicit in religious services like the above throughout Appalachia, numerous students of the region have highlighted the individualistic, fundamentalist, other-wordly, world-rejecting, emotional, and fatalistic characteristics of the religion:

> Religion is an individual matter just as are his other affairs. The purpose of the church in this life has seldom been other than to win souls to faith in a very personalistic way.[12]

> A people whose only experience for generations has been with

[12]Weller, *Yesterday's People*, 125.

a world of hard realities unadorned by the arts, eloquence, or imagination, it was inevitable that their folk churches should be founded upon fundamentalism of the starkest sort.[13]

Protracted meetings and funeral preachings in particular, are marked often by a high intensity of emotional expression. It is indeed the office of the preacher on such occasions to stir the audience to tears and repentance, and his success is measured somewhat by the extent to which he accomplishes this. The Highlander, moreover, is so accustomed to emotional preaching that he is wont to characterize the more restrained methods of foreign ministers as "not real religion."[14]

Out of the movements on the early frontier grew a highly informal church organization that still obtains through much of the region. The arrangement represents an adjustment by sparsely settled, economically poor, and familistic neighborhoods to meet their need for religious expression and periodic "renewal" of faith.[15]

As some of these passages suggest, religion in Appalachia has often been viewed in terms that suggest its meaning inheres in its function of providing an emotional catharsis or a means of self-assertion for individuals who are socially and economically powerless. As such, its relationship to the rest of society and culture in the region is negative, for its dominant characteristics—emotionalism, the focus on the individual, fatalism, and so forth—are not creative statements that somehow invest the world with particular meaning but rather are reflexes, a blind reaction to and rejection of the world.

Indigenous Meanings

Descriptive words and phrases like religious individualism,

[13]Caudill, *Night Comes to the Cumberlands*, 56.
[14]Campbell, *The Southern Highlander and His Homeland*, 183.
[15]Pearsall, *Little Smoky Ridge*, 115.

fatalism, and emotionalism aptly characterize one aspect of religious style on the top of the mountain. The informal and loosely structured nature of church services, for example, does appear to foster something like what Matthews has called "expressive" individualism;[16] since there is no well defined "right" time or way to offer a prayer, testimony, or hymn, individual members of the congregation are free and indeed are encouraged to inject much of their own emotions, styles, and interpretations into the service.

But these kinds of explanations do not necessarily reflect indigenous understandings. The congregations of the mountain's churches do not attribute individual spontaneity and emotionalism in church services to the individual but to the Holy Ghost. The explicit objective of the service is therefore not individual self-expression but getting "old Jim out of the way" so that the Spirit can "take control here and use the old mouthpiece." Members of the congregation are not encouraged to do and say whatever they like, but rather to do whatever they feel "called upon" to do. They are repeatedly admonished to "be obedient" and to "just let the Spirit take control." So when, as often happens, people jump to their feet during a service and shout "Praise Jesus!" or "Hallelujah!" they are not only expressing their own joy but also, and surely more importantly, acting as instruments of the Spirit.

These observations suggest that participants may well view the spontaneity and emotionalism of religious services less in terms of individual self-expression or self-assertion than in terms of self-negation. Each person is believed to enjoy an intimate relationship with a personal Savior, but this is anything but a relationship between equals. Although Christ is often spoken of as a "friend," who will aid and support each individual, He is also a potentially indwelling Holy Spirit, who will "take control" if people will but forget or efface themselves and thus permit it. In their religious services people

---

[16]Matthews, *Neighbor and Kin*, xxix-xxx.

try to create an atmosphere that is conducive not only to personal communion with God but also to loss of self, a necessary precondition for this communion.

The focal importance of self-negation to the religious experience is reflected in beliefs about conversion or salvation, the critical experience through which the individual comes into contact with the Holy and joins the family of Christ. One man, stirred by the sight of several church members working together constructing a new addition to the Cherokee Bluff Missionary Baptist Church, was moved to recall "the time when I got saved" in an emotional outburst that is here recounted as it was reconstructed from memory shortly after the event:

> Seeing this here church and all—reminds me of when I was just a boy and of that little mountain church where I got saved. Hallelujah! I was out running around with my friends one night like I used to do all the time before I accepted Christ. And I was coming home real late through the woods. And there was this terrible storm—thunder and lightning all around. And I was afraid and all a-shaking. And I cried out, "Save me, Jesus, save me, Jesus!" And He did, you know, right then and there! Praise the Lord! And I saw all of a sudden how sinful I had been and how all those things that used to matter to me don't really matter at all. And it was like I was a new person. Praise the Lord! I shouted with joy all the way home, and I been a Christian ever since, praise the Lord! It's such a great life with Jesus! Praise Jesus, praise Jesus!

While each conversion is considered to be a unique and very personal experience, residents' descriptions of their own conversions are similar in general structure to the account presented above. They usually include all or most of the following components:

(1) "And I saw all of a sudden how sinful I had been. . . ."—The suggestion or assertion that prior to conversion, the individual, whatever his or her former lifestyle or social position, had been "sinful" or "lost in sin."

(2) "I was afraid and all a-shaking. . . ."—A sudden awareness that he or she is alone and lost, usually accompanied by a sense of dread.

(3) "And I saw . . . how all those things that used to matter to me don't really matter at all. . . ."—A rejection of the individual's former worldly life.

(4) "And I cried out, 'Save me, Jesus, save me, Jesus!' And He did, right then and there. . . . And it was like I was a new person. . . ."—The experience of salvation itself, in which the convert's vision of the world and of his or her place in it is re-ordered.

Crucial to the conversion experience is repentance, the rejection of all the social and emotional trappings of the convert's former worldly life. Couched in an analytical framework similar to Arnold van Gennep's,[17] Bruce's description of the process of conversion in the "camp-meetings" of the antebellum South underlines the focal significance of the convert's separation from his or her pre-conversion life:

> . . . the first step in the actual conversion process, was conviction, involving a separation from the people who had been one's companions in that life and based on an acknowledgment of the world's wretchedness. Simultaneously there came to the sinner a knowledge of his own uncleanness and, hence, his unworthiness for a religious life. The potential convert was no longer what he had been, but neither was he what he hoped to become.
>
> This period of ambiguity constituted the most important aspect of the conversion experience, for it was a period when the structural framework of an individual's life was negated as he passed from one state or condition to another. Yet it was precisely during the unstructured period that the individual was enabled to come into contact with the divine.[18]

On the top of the mountain, people do not speak of a period

---

[17]*The Rites of Passage*, trans. Monika B. Vizedom and Gabrielle L. Caffee (Chicago: Univ. of Chicago Press, 1960).
[18]*And They All Sang Hallelujah*, 68-69.

110   We're All Kin

of "conviction," and they no longer make use of the "mourners' bench," where sinners under conviction used to pray for salvation. As one resident explained, the mourners' bench "was used more in the old days. When they had revivals the ones that was lost would kneel at it and the others would pray for them. I think it was called the mourners' bench because there was a lot of crying done at it—probably a lot like the Jews and their wailing wall. But it doesn't happen that way much anymore." Apparently, mountain residents' experiences of salvation do not or at least no longer entail a period of "mourning" or "conviction," conversion occuring almost simultaneously with the realization of being "lost in sin." Nonetheless, residents' accounts of conversion, their use of phrases like "born again" and "a new life" when speaking of salvation, and their insistence on adult baptism by complete immersion suggest that they conceive of salvation as critically entailing a rejection, repudiation, or "washing away" of all the individual's former values and relationships. Each person thus comes to Christ stripped of all those attributes that at least from a worldly perspective have made each one an individual.

The churches of the top of the mountain are indeed "individualistic" in their overriding concern with the individual soul and in the central importance assigned to the religious experience of the individual. But to equate this with an achievement-oriented individualism or even with Matthews' expressive individualism would be—to use an example from Clifford Geertz—like confusing winks and burlesqued winks: they may often look very much alike but the intents and imports are radically different.[19] The intimate relationship between each believer and his or her personal Savior is indeed the foundation and focus of the church service. But this relationship is marked less by a dialogue between each person

[19]"Thick Description: Toward an Interpretive Theory of Culture," in Geertz, *The Interpretation of Cultures: Selected Essays* (New York: Basic Books, 1973), 6-7.

and the Divine than by the individual's rebirth through voluntary submission to the will of the Holy Spirit.

The Homecoming

Although the churches of the top of the mountain stress the religious experience of the individual, the "Christian fellowship" of the church and the communal experience of the religious service is an important dimension of the religious life: ". . . sometimes them things get scattered out and you see one here and one over there. . . . But boys, when you get in the middle of it, something's gonna take place here now. So that's the way it is here tonight. . . . Come up here! Let's get closer together like we love one another."

Getting "closer together," getting "in the middle of it," is an important means of access to the Divine power. As Bruce notes of early Southern camp-meeting religion, "Most church members had received their initial supply of grace through conversion at a camp-meeting—that is, through participation in the activities of the community—and each could 'shake the manna tree' for a fresh supply whenever the saints gathered together."[20] On the mountain the church is more than a simple collectivity of believers. It is, as residents say, a "family of Christ," all members of which are bound together by their "Christian love" for one another. Although it is possible to be saved "without ever darkening the doors of the church house," participation—at least periodically—in this community of believers is important to most converts because it is one means of experiencing the Holy power, of creating an atmosphere conducive to letting "the Spirit take control" or to letting "something . . . take place here now."

The role and nature of this Christian fellowship, of getting

[20]*And They All Sang Hallelujah*, 120.

close together—what exactly it is that "takes place here now"—
are perhaps best addressed through a discussion of the annual
homecomings hosted by each family of the top of the mountain, for it is at these events more than at any other kind of
religious gathering that the unity of the family of Christ is
realized.

A homecoming is a day-long family and religious event; it
includes a morning sermon, an afternoon "singing," a grave
decoration, and a covered dish dinner. Each family's homecoming is presided over by a guest preacher invited for the
occasion and is celebrated in the community church and the
cemetery where the family's ancestors are buried. The Johnsons of Rocky Gap and the Bradleys hold their homecomings
respectively in the Rocky Gap Baptist Church and the Cherokee Bluff Missionary Baptist Church and the cemeteries adjacent to each. The Campbells have recently converted an
abandoned one-room schoolhouse near their cemetery to the
"Mountain Home Church" which, except for an occasional
Easter morning service, is used primarily for homecomings.
The Johnsons of Mine Flats celebrate their homecoming in
their family and community cemetery, and they have built
next to it permanent tables of rough pine planks for the covered dish dinner that always accompanies this event.

At around nine o'clock in the morning on the Sunday of
the homecoming, people begin to arrive at the cemetery to
place bunches of flowers on the graves of their departed kin.
The service itself begins around ten o'clock and opens as do
all religious services with congregational singing. Following
this, a message is delivered by the guest preacher. The usual
subject of the homecoming message is heaven and the eventual
heavenly reunion of all family members. The following text
is from the message delivered at the 1976 Campbell family
homecoming:

> We want to talk about our future home, our heavenly home,
> the place where we'll go when life is over. . . . Now John is
> telling us just a little bit about it—what heaven is gonna be

like. Now I've tried, over a period of years I've tried to picture that heaven. I've read about it in the Bible . . . and the people, we all sing about heaven. But there's no way that I can get enough words together, there's no way that I can say—and I'm trying to tell you just how great that heaven is gonna be. . . . Now we all know as far as this life, this life comes to an end. And we all know that there's not one of us here that's not some day or another gonna have to face death. But the Bible tells us here in this scripture that I have just read, in this city that John said he looked up and saw coming down, he said there won't be no death. . . .

We live in a world today where there's fears and doubts. I would say there's not a person here, in this congregation today, where there's not been some kind of a problem in your life . . . something is troubling you. A Christian life is not always easy. Just because we say that we're saved, that don't mean that it's always easy. There's many fears and doubts, and there's many things that we meet here in this life that we don't understand. . . . But one of these days we're gonna be safe at home with Jesus. It's been said anymore in your own home that you're not safe. And it's true . . . but in heaven it's not gonna be like that. There's not gonna be no death, there won't be. . . . We're gonna be able to live forever and praise the Lord!

Old Carl down the road—everybody knows Carl—once he said to me, "Preacher, what do you think people are gonna do when they get to heaven, what they gonna do up there?" I says, "Well, the best way that I know to describe it is this: just wait till I get there and I been there about ten thousand years and I think I can tell you more about it!"

You know, in heaven people say we're gonna do a lot of things. In heaven people say they're gonna shout forever. Well, I believe we'll shout all right. But we're not gonna be shouting all the time. You've heard people say, well, I'm gonna sing forever. Well, I don't believe we'll be singing all the time. But the Bible does teach us in heaven we're gonna be there together forever and forever and forevermore. And as far as singing— we all know that there's gonna be a great choir, a great *heavenly* choir. My, my, we can just think about the people that's gonna sing in that choir. And you've heard a lot of people say, a lot of ministers say, and I'll have to say that I'm one of them, that here in this life we can't sing, we just can't sing at all. But in heaven I believe that everyone, and I may be wrong but I believe in heaven that everybody is gonna be able to sing. I do, I do. I believe that everybody will be able to sing. We'll all be singing together in that heavenly choir. And while we're singing together here in this heavenly choir we won't have to think about any problems—we can just keep on singing in that heavenly choir. Keep on singing, and that's forever and forevermore!

In heaven we'll all be singing! And there won't be no death, won't be no death. In heaven we won't have to say goodbye. I look out here in this old graveyard and I think about all those that have gone on before, that we've had to say goodbye to. I know probably each one of you has got someone buried out there—maybe a father or a mother or a brother or a sister. But in heaven we won't have to say goodbye, there won't be no more death, no more sorrow. We'll all be together again, and that's forever!

. . . in this place that I'm talking about, it's gonna be a land of perfect peace. I know one of these days the Lord is gonna call for me and the Lord is gonna call for you, and we're all gonna go to a land, a land where there's gonna be perfect peace. We're gonna be together forever and evermore. There won't be no sorrow over there, no, there won't be. All the sorrow will be over. The Bible says in heaven there won't be no more crying. There won't be no more separation. And that's something to look forward to, that's something to praise the Lord for, that's something to shout about! 'Cause in heaven we're gonna be together, we're gonna sing together in that heavenly choir!

As this excerpt illustrates, heaven is depicted as a place that is completely other than the earthly world, a place that is marked by what this world is not. In other words, it is a land where there will be no sorrow, no trouble, no death. But heaven does have at least one positive attribute: everyone will be together in a "great heavenly choir," where they will be able to "sing and shout" forever.

This heavenly singing and shouting is an activity that has an analogue, however imperfect, in the congregational singing of the earthly church. Although people can't really and truly "sing" in this world, they can begin to experience something of "what heaven is gonna be like" through participation in the singing and shouting of the religious service. It is to these activities that the afternoon of the homecoming is devoted. While the morning events—the grave decoration and sermon, followed by a covered dish dinner—are attended mainly by members of the host family and community, residents and nonresidents who have close kin buried in the cemetery where the homecoming is being held, the afternoon "singing" often attracts much larger crowds of people who have come because they "like to sing and shout." Many of these afternoon participants are singers and instrumentalists from other churches throughout the local mountain area. They are known for their ability to inspire singings with the collective emotional abandon that is so highly sought after for these events. When this is achieved, as it often is at homecomings, members of the congregation begin to jump to their feet to "shout," crying "Praise Jesus!" "Hallelujah!" "I'm glad I'm saved!" Most are in tears, but people say their tears are tears of joy and happiness. Their joy is infectious, and at the emotional height of the singing more and more people may join in the shouting, raising their voices in praise of the Lord and in anticipation of the joys of heaven.

The singing and shouting of the homecoming and the far more joyous heavenly singing and shouting that it anticipates celebrates a sense of spiritual unity with others, a sense of each person being filled with the one Spirit, and it derives much of its emotional power from this. Although salvation and heaven are spoken of in terms of individual happiness and fulfillment, a sense of community—of belonging, as Bruce

states, to "an eternal community, stretching backward to include God's first 'chosen people' and forward to eternity"[21]—
is an important dimension of this happiness, an integral part
of conversion and the religious experience. Membership in
this eternal community is open to all, for all that is required
is acceptance of Christ's offer of salvation. Through this acceptance people are reborn and come to see the world in new
terms. In this new world people not only enjoy an intimate
and comforting relationship with a personal Savior, but also
see themselves to be spiritually one with all other believers.
The potential for this spiritual unity has been there all along—
Christ's offer of salvation is universal—but to be realized it
has to be recognized and accepted by each person. The conversion experience, in which the individual suddenly sees that
"all those things that used to matter to me don't really matter
at all," in which worldly values, meanings, and distinctions
are swept aside, permits and constitutes the recognition of this
underlying unity and oneness.

Although the focus of much of the homecoming service is
on death and heavenly reunion, "death" and "heaven" may
connote more than a future event and abode. Bruce has remarked of the apparent emphasis on death in camp-meeting
religion:

> The death of which they sang was a symbolic death indicative
> of the sharpness of that break with the old life which had to
> precede the new. . . . As earthly death was necessary to the
> assumption of eternal life in heaven, so was death of the sinful
> self a prior condition to the beginning of the new life of as-
> surance. The death talk of the choruses was less a wish for an
> event than a symbol of the kind of radical break with worldly
> life that conversion required.[22]

As death may be a metaphor for rebirth, so heaven may represent a vision of the new world that is hoped to be attained

[21]Ibid., 116.
[22]Ibid., 105-6.

on this earth through conversion, a world where "we're gonna be together" and "sing together" in a "great choir." The emphasis on death and heaven that marks the homecoming and many other kinds of religious services on the mountain may be less a fatalistic and resigned response to impoverished circumstances or powerlessness than a creative response to the world and its problems and contradictions (like death), a restructuring of the world in religious terms.

This new world, however, can never be fully attained on earth. As the preacher at the Campbell homecoming put it, "here in this life we can't sing, we just can't sing at all." Despite their conversions and rebirths, believers are still enmeshed in a "sinful" world that imposes artificial barriers between the individual and the Divine and between the individual and all other persons. Although these barriers can periodically be overcome and the spiritual unity of the family of Christ can begin to be realized at religious gatherings, this realization is transitory and it is always imperfect.

It is imperfect in at least two senses. First, it can only approximate the total joy believers look forward to in the afterlife, a joy that is so unknown and unattainable on earth that "there's no way I can get enough words together" to describe it. And it is imperfect, secondly, in the sense that it cannot, on earth, encompass the entire family of Christ. Not only are the living separated from the dead, but the sense of community, of spiritual unity, that believers seek can most often be realized only among relatively small groups of the living, among people who are close to one another in this life and therefore have relatively few barriers between them to overcome. The sense of unity that pervades religious gatherings most often derives from and is the intimacy and closeness of a small group.

The Earthly Family and the Family of Christ

It is in the light of this limitation that the relationships between earthly family groups and the "family of Christ" should
be considered.

As seen, mountain residents view the family as a group of
individuals who are united by their essential similarities to one
another. This unity and the similarities on which it is founded
are "natural," deriving from the shared biological substance
or "blood" inherited from a common ancestor. Yet while the
family is a fact of nature, its realization depends on the will
or assent of the individual, for those who do not behave toward one another as kin, those who do not stick together, are
not "really" kin. The members of a family recognize and assent to their underlying natural unity and hence actualize their
bonds of kinship with one another. They are those who, rec-
ognizing their common kinship, behave toward one another
as equals and at the same time respect and foster the integrity
of the individual—within the family "it's not what you are
but who you are" that is important.

Of necessity, such a group is limited in size. The intimate
solidarity, what Schneider has called "enduring diffuse solidarity,"[23] that is expressed in the symbol of shared blood
cannot encompasss large numbers of people, for it is founded
on personal intimacies of the sort that arise from the day-to-
day interactions of close neighbors and kinfolk. While on one
level "we're all kin," members of "one big family," on another level some kinfolk are closer than others.

Residents' conceptions of the unity of the family group have
many affinities with their conceptions of the unity of the
"family of Christ." As the family group is composed of those
who recognize and assent to their underlying and natural similarities and bonds, so the family of Christ is composed of
those who have accepted Christ and have thereby apprehended

[23]*American Kinship*, 50ff.

their essential unity with all other believers. This Christian unity is a spiritual bond that is inherent not in human nature but rather in the relationship between man and God. Like the natural unity of the family group, however, it has to be consciously embraced by the individual to be realized. In the light of these similarities, the association between families and churches and more particularly the family focus of the homecoming is hardly surprising. For it is within the context of the small family group composed of individuals who are "close" to one another that believers can begin to experience the kind of spiritual unity that they seek.

This experience undoubtedly serves to promote the solidarity of the family group. Yet while the churches of the top of the mountain often appear to replicate and legitimize the social order in a Durkheimian fashion and to promote a sense of unity with others, which is also very Durkheimian, a religion is more than a social glue. Geertz's definition perhaps provides one of the most comprehensive expressions of its meaning and role: ". . . a religion is (1) a system of symbols which acts to (2) establish powerful, pervasive, and long-lasting moods and motivations in men by (3) formulating conceptions of a general order of existence and (4) clothing these conceptions with such an aura of factuality that (5) the moods and motivations seem uniquely realistic."[24]

Although a religion often or perhaps even usually may serve to legitimize and perpetuate a particular social order, Geertz's definition suggests that it deals less with the particularities of a society than with a particular vision of social and human generalities. It provides its adherents with a coherent way of looking at and being in the world, a way that, while it derives from, lends coherence to, and indeed plays a part in fashioning the givens of a particular time and place, transcends that time and place to address what it posits as fundamental and uni-

---

[24]"Religion As a Cultural System," in *Anthropological Approaches to the Study of Religion*, ed. Michael Banton (London: Tavistock Publications, 1966); rpt. Geertz, *The Interpretation of Cultures*, 90.

versal human truths about "a general order of existence," about life, personhood, and human interrelatedness.

Viewed from this perspective, it is less the family that is the object of religious attention at the homecoming than the idea of the family. Although church members speak of themselves as "brothers and sisters in Christ" and talk of their "brotherly love" for one another and although the homecoming in particular appears to celebrate the unity of the family, the "family" and the "brotherly love" of which residents speak at religious gatherings extend far beyond the boundaries of any earthly family. While the homecoming is said to be "sort of like a family reunion" at which family members "get together in the name of the Lord," still everyone is invited, and the best homecomings are those that attract large numbers of people from throughout the local region. When all of these "brothers and sisters in Christ" get together to "sing and shout" they can begin to apprehend their fundamental kinship with one another, and some of the import of the fact that "we're all kin" can be experienced. That they cannot all get closer together enduringly and in larger numbers, that the new world that is envisioned in the concept of heaven cannot be perfectly realized on earth is due to the frailty of human beings and the imperfections of the world.

CONCLUSION

Conclusion

In speaking of families, residents of the top of the mountain stress the equality, similarity, and fundamental unity of all family members, a unity that is "natural" because it derives from the fact of shared blood inherited from a common ancestor. Communities, in contrast, are often spoken of in terms that stress the individuality and freedom of their residents. While families appear to be immutable, naturally ascribed groups, communities are fluid and voluntary groups.

The fact that family and community memberships tend to coincide, coupled with the finding that there is little or no apparent genealogical rationale for the demarcation of four family groups, might easily be interpreted as suggesting that the family groups of the top of the mountain may "really" be residence groups whose members often conceptualize their relationships to one another in terms of kinship. Thus, communities become identified with a world of actions, statistical regularities, and patterns of behavior while families are identified with a world of thought, ideas, and perceptions, a dichotomy that has often been expressed as a distinction between social organization or structure on the one hand and culture on the other.

This kind of interpretation, while it has for long enjoyed a widespread popularity in the social sciences, is fraught with difficulties. For one thing, as applied to the top of the mountain in the manner suggested, it entails a highly arbitrary selection and categorization of the ethnographic data. There is, quite simply, nothing in what residents say of families and communities to suggest that they belong to different orders of reality. Aside from the initial problem of separating ideas from action, of deciding just what aspects of a diverse ethnographic totality pertain to culture and what aspects pertain to social organization, this type of analysis tends to lead to the suggestion of a logically untenable disjunction or incongruity between what are, according to Geertz, "but different abstractions from the same phenomena."[1]

Let us recall, for example, two particular cases of social conflict on the top of the mountain: the quarrel between the Johnsons of Rocky Gap and the Bradleys that led to the establishment of the Rocky Gap Baptist Church and the dispute within the Johnson family of Rocky Gap over the unequal division of "family land" among a small number of individual land owners. Are not both clear instances of conflict and social tension arising from a clash between ideological systems and systems of action? In the former case it would appear that the split within the Cherokee Bluff Missionary Baptist Church occurred as a result of an incompatibility between a real world situation of personal clashes and enmities and an indigenous notion of a church as a unified "family of Christ" whose members are bound to one another by ties of "brotherly" and "Christian" love. By leaving the Cherokee Bluff Missionary Baptist Church and establishing their own independent congregation, the Johnsons brought the real world into alignment with their ideas about the world. In the latter case, which is yet to be resolved, it appears that the source of the dispute is

[1]"Ritual and Social Change: A Javanese Example," *American Anthropologist* 61 (1959); rpt. Geertz, *The Interpretation of Cultures*, 145.

a discrepancy between the idea that each community is composed of family land and the fact of individual land ownership and control.

To some extent these interpretations are undoubtedly correct, and I have commented on both cases in very similar terms. But the analytical framework here employed, one that rather arbitrarily identifies one part of the total situation with *ideas* about what is and another part with what *in fact* is, must, if carried to its logical end, lead to the conclusion that the people of the top of the mountain are mad or at best seriously deluding themselves. For how else could their implied failure to perceive and account for the facts that people sometimes dislike one another and that people own land as individuals (remember, within the framework of this theory these are the data of behavior, of what the world is, not of what people think the world is) possibly be explained?

Of course, residents of the top of the mountain not only own their land individually, disposing of it or refusing to dispose of it in whatever manner they see fit, and often harbor unbrotherly feelings toward one another, but also have a lively appreciation of these facts: they are the data of both thought and behavior. In fact, how could it be otherwise, how could these disputes possibly have occurred if people did not perceive and have thoughts, for example, about both family land and individual land tenures? The apparent incongruities and discrepancies in these cases are not between a social organization or behavioral pattern based exclusively on individual land tenures and voluntary groupings on the one hand and a cultural or conceptual framework that views the world exclusively in terms of family land and naturally ascribed bonds of family solidarity on the other. The problem here lies more in the inevitable internal inadequacies of the cultural framework itself, of the patterns and significances that people perceive in their and others' behavior and in terms of which they respond to it.

Geertz has recently discussed the ethnographic enterprise as follows:

> Once human behavior is seen as . . . symbolic action—action which, like phonation in speech, pigment in painting, line in writing, or sonance in music, signifies—the question as to whether culture is patterned conduct or a frame of mind, or even the two somehow mixed together, loses sense. The thing to ask about a burlesqued wink or a mock sheep raid is not what their ontological status is. It is the same as that of rocks on the one hand and dreams on the other—they are things of this world. The thing to ask is what their import is: what it is . . . that, in their occurrence and through their agency, is getting said.[2]

For Geertz, then, anthropology consists in "explicating [other peoples'] explications."[3] Culture is "not a power, something to which social events, behaviors, institutions, or processes can be causally attributed," but rather "a context, something within which they can be intelligibly . . . described."[4]

My approach to the analysis of the top of the mountain has been more in the nature of "explicating explications," of trying to understand and make sense out of what people there say and do in terms of their own contexts of meanings and perceptions, than in that of counterpoising what is to what people think it is.

When I began fieldwork on the top of the mountain in 1974, I was struck by the omnipresence of kinship. Not only was it said that everyone (or at least almost everyone) was related to everyone else, but people seemed to make a great deal of this circumstance in their daily talk and behavior. Where one lived, who one's friends were, where one went to church, where one was finally buried—all were a function of one's position in the local kinship network, or so it seemed.

---

[2]"Thick Description: Toward an Interpretive Theory of Culture," in *The Interpretation of Cultures*, 10.

[3]Ibid., 9.

[4]Ibid., 14.

Later, when genealogies had been duly collected, the role of kinship—which had initially seemed so clear and straightforward—became increasingly problematic. For these genealogies revealed that everyone was indeed related to everyone else (or almost), but in so many complex and overlapping ways as to make kinship in itself appear to be quite useless for the patterning and understanding of interpersonal behavior and the demarcation of social groups. Not only did the genealogies reveal no "natural" basis for the grouping or categorization of kin, residents themselves did not seem to use any cultural categories or distinctions (except that between "close" and "distant" kin, neither of which anyone was able to define, or indeed seemed interested in defining, with any precision or clarity) by which all these kinfolk might be sorted out. In fact, not only were there no exotic categories—"patrilineal" vs. "matrilateral" kin, for example—even such standard genealogical distinctions as that of generation were often muted or ignored in the terminological system of address: everyone—grandparents and grandchildren, brothers and sisters, parents and children, uncles and aunts, nephews and nieces—frequently addressed one another as "buddy." It appeared that culture and actual behavior were two very different things, that however much people liked to talk about kinship, it had no real significance for the patterning and therefore for the understanding of their daily lives.

This initial interpretation was wrong, of course. The difficulty lay in uncritically applying my own idea of kinship (or rather a widely held anthropological conception of kinship—my own ideas upon reflection would probably be closer to those of the people of the top of the mountain) to the definition and analysis of the problem. This conception of kinship holds that it pertains exclusively to the facts of consanguinity and affinity. Schneider cites Marion Levy's defintiion of kinship as providing a particularly lucid illustration of this: "[Kinship structure is] that portion of the total institutionalized structure of a society that, in addition to other orientations, sometimes equally if not even more important, determines the membership of its units and the nature of the solidarity among its members by orientation to the facts of biological relatedness and/or sexual intercourse."[5] This definition suggests that kinship is something that exists out there in the real world in its own right and is therefore an immutable given that the anthroplogist records and analyzes and the natives, however strangely they may categorize their kinfolk, simply adhere to in their dealings with one another. And if they sometimes do not adhere to it very faithfully, then it is "classificatory" kinship, suggesting that it is somehow different from "real" kinship, which pertains to the facts of blood and marriage.

As Schneider has been at some pains to explain, although biological relatedness, copulation, parturition, and so forth certainly exist out there in the real world, kinship as a *cultural construct* in terms of which people understand and explicate social groupings and relationships is whatever the natives say it is. And, it should be added, in some places (most, according to Schneider) the natives might have little or nothing to say about it, in which case it would behoove anthropologists to direct their attention elsewhere or at least frame the analysis in different terms.[6]

Now it so happens that the particular natives with which we are here concerned seem to be in agreement with the anthropologists. They say that kinship is a matter of biology, of the shared blood inherited from a common ancestor and of the "natural" similarities among kinfolk that are attributed to the fact of shared blood. But while biology and blood are the *sine qua non* of kinship, the distinguishing feature that sets a kinship relationship apart from all other kinds of relation-

[5]Cited in David M. Schneider, "Kinship and Biology," in *Aspects of the Analysis of Family Structure*, ed. Ainsley J. Coale et al. (Princeton: Princeton Univ. Press, 1965), 83.

[6]For the fullest exposition of this argument, see "What Is Kinship All About?" in *Kinship Studies*, ed. Reining, 32-63.

ships, kinship is rather more than a simple matter of biology. For as the term "blood" is used by residents of the top of the mountain when speaking of kinship, it connotes more than a particular red substance—it connotes a kind of social relationship between those who share it, a relationship that Schneider has described as "love" or "enduring diffuse solidarity"[7] and that residents of the mountain speak of as "sticking together through thick and thin." Blood is thus both a substance and a symbol for the kind of social relationship that its sharing is believed to entail.

This relationship based on shared blood has two aspects: on the one hand, it entails a relationship of identity, similarity, or equality. Kinfolk, because they share the blood inherited from a common ancestor, are very like one another, and the more blood they have in common—that is, the closer their genealogical relationship—then the greater their similarities are believed to be. And it is because of these similarities, because they are of the "same flesh and blood," that kinfolk "naturally" love and support one another. On the other hand, however, the love that kinfolk feel toward one another is not only compelled by biology, by the facts of nature, it is also given freely and voluntarily. Kinfolk like one another as persons, as unique individuals, and the suggestion that their love for one another might have nothing to do with personal feelings would undoubtedly strike mountain residents as being both appalling and contrary to experience. It is asserted, in fact, that within the family, within the group of close kin, people are most free to "be themselves," to act in accordance with their personal feelings and inclinations.

In the light of these conceptions, the relevance of kinship to the social organization of the top of the mountain becomes intelligible. Residents speak of their neighborhood in terms of four "families"—the Campbells, the Johnsons of Rocky Gap, the Bradleys, and the Johnsons of Mine Flats—and four "com-

[7]*American Kinship*, 50ff.

munitites"—Campbell Flats, Rocky Gap, Bradley Flats, and
Mine Flats. A family is described as a group of "close" kin
who are related to one another by the bonds of shared blood
inherited from a common ancestor. A community, on the
other hand, is composed of the people who live in a particular
area. But you often cannot tell who belongs or does not belong to a particular family by consulting a genealogy—and
residents have never claimed that you could. Nor can you
always tell which households belong to which communities
by consulting an aerial photograph—someone has to explain
where one community ends and another begins. For families
are not identical to species or genera and communities are not
geographical regions or areas. They are both social groupings—that is, human creations—whose members are bound
to one another not by the physical facts of genealogical or
geographical propinquity but rather by the imports or meanings that people attach to these facts.

By and large, family members define their relationship to
one another by reference to descent from a common ancestor.
Community residents, again by and large, are those who have
inherited rights to the family land of the community, rights
that are based on their descent from the family and community founder. But while the idioms employed, those of descent
and inheritance, are similar, both pointing back to kinship,
they stress different kinds of inheritance and different aspects
of the indigenous conception of kinship. Family membership
is based on blood and on the natural and involuntary kind of
inheritance that anthropologists speak of as descent. The
"family land" of which each community is composed, however, is inherited through being "passed on" and accepted
through the voluntary acts of particular individuals. While
people are born into families, they move into (and out of)
communities.

Of course, the differences between families and communities are not as great as this contrast implies. People are not
only born into families, for example, they also marry into

them. And although the blood ties that unite family members are facts of nature, they must also be validated through human agency. Within limits the closeness of the kinship bond is defined as much by reference to personal affinities as to genealogical connection. Those who do not behave in an appropriate manner, that is, those who do not "stick together through thick and thin," are not "really" kin, or at least not "close" kin, members of the same family group.

The notion of a community as a voluntary group is similarly qualified. Although family land is owned by individuals and is passed on or not passed on in accordance with the wishes of these individuals, the idea that it is 'family land" conditions and influences their acts and decisions. While the individual is free to do as he or she sees fit, it is only natural that people should choose to reside with their closest kin and sell or give their land to them, both because they like them or feel closest to them and because these are the people who "got rights" to it. The point is that what is stressed in residents' descriptions of families—blood, ascription, natural similarities and identities, and the bonds that derive from these—are muted when residents speak of communities. And conversely, what is stressed in comments on communities—voluntarism, individual free will, living in a community because, among other things, you like it there or you "feel freer" there—is muted within the context of the family.

Blood and family land—genealogies and geography—do not so much create families and communities as they express them. A family is a group of people who talk about their relationships to one another in terms of shared blood, descent from a common ancestor, and family traits. They love and support one another because they are very like one another and it is therefore "natural" for them to do so. A community is a group of people who talk about their relationships to one another in terms of rights, duties, acts, and decisions associated with the passing on of family land. They love and support one another not so much because they are very like one another as because they like one another. Being like one another, being of the same flesh and blood, and liking one another as perons is, to borrow Schneider's phrase, what "kinship is all about" on the top of the mountain. When residents say that "we're all kin," they are saying something not only about the fact of genealogical connections but also and more importantly about what those connections signify for them.

The ideas and assumptions embodied in this conception of kinship receive their fullest expression in the religious symbol system, particularly that complex of ideas and symbols that center about and inform the notion of salvation, the ultimate end to which all religious activities are directed. Christ's offer of salvation is both universal and particular. While open to all, it is a personal offer made to each individual. What is required is acceptance, a freely made individual decision. What is gained is an experience of the Divine, of the Spirit that potentially dwells within each individual and unites them in "brotherly" or "Christian" love, and a vision of "what heaven is gonna be like," a place where "we'll all be together" and be able to "sing and shout forever."

This experience and this vision, however, are not mirror images, expressed in religious terms, of people's experiences and visions of the earthly world. God and heaven are not society writ large. Conceptions of the Divine, of heaven and salvation, obviously draw upon the perceptions and experiences of people in society. But they go beyond these to address human potentialities, potentialities that are inherent in man's nature and in the relationship between man and God but that in this "sinful" world cannot be fully realized. Although residents' visions of heaven are "things of this world," as Geertz has said, they are not about only this world because "in this world we can't sing, we just can't sing at all."

While religion posits that all human beings are equal and united, that the "family of Christ" is indeed the family of man, it also asserts that the realization of their fundamental unity depends on individual volition. By nature mankind is one, but people also have free wills. It is by virtue of their exercise of this freedom that they not only can experience the Divine but also fall into sin.

While on the one hand "we're all kin," on the other some kin are indisputably closer than others, bound to one another by a love that is both natural, or compelled by their inner natures, and freely given. These ideas of natural unity and individual freedom derive from and shape people's perceptions of their experiences in their families and communities and thus inform and explicate these groups. It is in their religious beliefs and services that the people of the top of the mountain seek to fully unify these conceptions and experiences and to create a world in which human beings are indeed united in a universal and freely chosen "Christian love" for one another. It is not happenstance that their fullest experience of this world should occur in the setting of small churches whose congregations are composed of close kin and in the setting of homecomings that draw on the unity of the family group to express the spiritual unity of the family of Christ.

As has been noted in the introductory chapter, my analysis and conclusions concerning what "kinship is all about" on the top of the mountain closely parallel the work of David Schneider for American kinship in general. In *American Kinship: A Cultural Account*, Schneider discusses the American conception of kinship as being compounded of two principles or "orders":

> . . . the cultural universe of relatives in American kinship is constructed from two major cultural orders, the *order of nature* and the *order of law*. Relatives in *nature* share heredity. Relatives *in law* are bound only by law or custom, by the code for conduct, by the pattern for behavior. They are relatives by virtue of their *relationship*, not their biogenetic attributes.[8]

Schneider describes the relationship "in nature," that based on shared heredity or blood, as follows:

[8]Ibid., 27.

> A blood relationship is a relationship of identity, they [the
> natives] believe. This is expressed as "being of the same flesh
> and blood." It is a belief in common biological constitution,
> and aspects like temperament, build, physiognomy, and habits
> are noted as signs of this shared biological make-up, this special
> identity of relatives with each other.[9]

He then contrasts the blood relationship with the relationship
in law in terms of voluntary vs. involuntary, subjective vs.
objective, permanent vs. terminable, and so forth. According
to Schneider, the relatives *par excellence* are the blood relatives
(or, as people on the mountain would say, the "close" blood
relatives)—those who are related both by nature and by relationship or code for conduct. As I have expressed it, they
are those who love and support one another both because it
is in their nature to do so and because they like one another
as persons.

Yet while, as the passages cited above illustrate, my analysis
of the top of the mountain is in many ways similar to Schneider's analysis of American kinship, it also diverges from his
work and his approach in many respects. Three of the most
general and fundamental of these merit brief discussion here.

The first concerns the nature and role of affinity and its
relation to the notion of blood ties. While Schneider has based
his discussion on the cultural distinction between blood relatives, or relatives in nature, and affines, or relatives in law, I
have said very little about affines, instead focusing upon the
distinction between families composed of people who have
inherited blood from a common ancestor and communities
composed of people who have inherited rights to family land
from the same common ancestor. The role of conceptions
regarding affinity on the mountain did not (and still does not)
seem to me to be particularly crucial to an understanding of
the import of the statement that "we're all kin." No doubt,
this is related in part to the prevalence of endogamy. On the

[9]Ibid., 25.

mountain, many or most of your affines are your blood kin anyway—the saying that "like marries like" has a more literal import here than in many other parts of the United States— and the distinction between affinity and consanguinity seemed to have little direct bearing on residents' understandings of those particular aspects of their social world with which I have here been concerned.

This is not to suggest that residents of the top of the mountain do not, like other Americans, distinguish between relatives by blood and relatives by marriage. But I confess to profound uncertainties regarding the nature and import of this distinction. Although Schneider defines the relationship in law as being viewed as both a terminable relationship and as one of enduring love, in the main he focuses on the contrast between blood and marriage, nature and law, cognatic love and conjugal love in terms of polar opposites. Residents of the mountain, however, at least within the context of their discussions and comments regarding families, tend less to contrast relatives by blood and relatives by marriage than to focus on their similarities.

Aside from the substantive issue of affinity, the approach used here differs from Schneider's in its orientation to the conception of culture. Throughout his recent work, Schneider has been concerned with the study of culture as an analytically isolable system of symbols and meanings. To this end he distinguishes "culture," as a widely shared and very general and fundamental system of symbols and meanings, from norms, which are "patterns for action" that are "much more specific, at a narrower degree of generality, more restricted in scope and context, and not widely shared outside of a particular social field":

> What is widely shared and what has a high level of generality may not be the norm so much as the cultural aspects of the norm. This becomes especially true when the norm is misstated in very general terms rather than in its full detail, as for instance, when one says that the role of the mother in the

American family should be nurturant. Such a statement does not specify how to be nurturant, how the mother should act when she is being nurturant, what "to be nurturant" entails. It is insufficient to define the norm for the mother in the American family in such terms. How a rich mother should be nurturant is normatively different from how a poor mother should be nurturant; it is different for middle-class and lower-class mothers, for devout Catholic and devout Jewish mothers . . . toward a first child or a last child, and so on. Hence the term "nurturant" is more a cultural than a normative designation, and it is widely understandable because a variety of somewhat different normative prescriptions may be attached to it.[10]

Considered in this way, culture becomes Geertz's "models of" the world, but very general ones, "a body of definitions, premises, statements, postulates, presumptions, propositions, and perceptions about the nature of the universe and man's place in it."[11] Norms, on the other hand, are "models for"[12] acting in the world; while they are shaped by cultural premises and first principles and while these principles are indeed derived largely from them, norms partake of the details and conditions of a specific and limited social field.

In contrast to Schneider's concerns, mine here have been with just such a specific social field. Like him, I have argued that this field is best understood within and through the framework of culture. Here, however, culture has not been restricted to mean primarily or only the most general "models of." For aside from the practical difficulties of separating the general "model of" aspect of many kinds of statements from their more delimited "model for" aspect, restricting the use

---

[10]"Notes Toward a Theory of Culture," in *Meaning in Anthropology*, ed. Keith H. Basso and Henry A. Selby (Albuquerque: Univ. of New Mexico Press, 1976), 201-2.

[11]Ibid., 203.

[12]Geertz's distinction between "models of" and "models for" is set forth in "Religion as a Cultural System," in *Anthropological Approaches to the Study of Religion*, ed. Banton; rpt. Geetz, *The Interpretation of Cultures*.

of the term "culture" in this way could be misleading here, implying that most of the details and shadings of the families, communities, and churches on the mountain—the "relatively specific situations" to which norms pertain and by which Schneider distinguishes norms from culture—can somehow exist apart from any cultural formulation of them. While it is true that Edward B. Tylor's definition of culture as "that complex whole" has little utility, I have found it useful for my analytic purposes here to provisionally treat culture more broadly—and less rigorously—than Schneider does, viewing it as shared understandings, indigenously perceived patterns and significances of (and for) very specific words and actions and the formulations and understandings—at whatever level of generality or specificity—that these imply.

A final major difference between my analysis of the top of the mountain and Schneider's work on American kinship relates to the goals of our respective inquiries. Schneider has often been concerned with delineating the American conception of kinship as a cultural domain that is distinguished from other cultural domains. What is it, in other words, that for Americans distinguishes a relationship of kinship from an economic relationship, for example, or a relationship of friendship? My concern, in contrast, has not been with distinguishing kinship from other domains but rather with understanding how, on the top of the mountain, social relationships in general are understood and shaped in terms of indigenous conceptions of kinship.

It is not that residents of the mountain do not view kinship as a particular kind of relationship, different from other kinds of social relationships. They do—else why would they have a word for it?[13] But I think this distinction (and, I suspect,

---

[13]Schneider, however, has concluded since writing *American Kinship* that the American system of symbols and meanings pertaining to kinship "was not isomorphic with any such category, but instead spread far beyond its boundaries" and that "kinship, nationality, religion, education, and the whole sex-role system were all parts of the same cultural galaxy."

that between consanguinity and affinity) may have more relevance to their understanding of the differences between their own neighborhood and the wider American society in which all of them participate to one extent or another. This, however, is another topic. My concern has been with the small world of the top of the mountain, a place where "we're all kin," and where kinship, depending on the approach adopted and depending on what the natives make of it, is therefore either everything or nothing.

("Notes Toward a Theory of Culture," in *Meaning in Anthropology*, ed. Basso and Selby, 210 and 211. See also Schneider, "Kinship, Nationality, and Religion in American Culture: Toward a Definition of Kinship," in *Forms of Symbolic Action*, ed. Robert F. Spencer, American Ethnological Society [Seattle: Univ. of Washington Press, 1969].) This is very suggestive, particularly in light of the material presented here, but it tends to locate "culture" at such a high level of generality as to make it almost as problematic for ethnographic purposes as Tylor's definition.

BIBLIOGRAPHY

Alexander, Jack. "The Cultural Domain of Marriage," *American Ethnologist* 5 (Feb. 1978), 5-14.

Banton, Michael, ed. *Anthropological Approaches to the Study of Religion*. London: Tavistock Publications, 1966.

Batteau, Allen. "The American Culture of Appalachia." Paper presented at the American Anthropological Association Meetings, Cincinnati, Nov.-Dec. 1979.

_____. "Appalachia and the Concept of Culture: A Theory of Shared Misunderstandings," *Appalachian Journal* 7, No. 1-2, Special Issue, "Process, Policy, and Context: Contemporary Perspectives on Appalachian Culture" (Autumn-Winter 1979-80), 9-31.

_____. "Modernization: Inflections on the Appalachian Kinship System." Unpublished paper.

Billings, Dwight. "Culture and Poverty in Appalachia: A Theoretical Discussion and Empirical Analysis," *Social Forces* 53 (Dec. 1974). Rpt. in *Appalachia: Social Context Past and Present*. Ed. Bruce Ergood and Bruce E. Kuhre. Dubuque, Iowa: Kendall/Hunt, 1976.

Brewer, Earl D. C. "Religion and the Churches." In *The

Southern Appalachian Region: A Survey. Ed. Thomas R. Ford. Lexington: Univ. of Kentucky Press, 1962.

Brown, James Stephen. "The Conjugal Family and the Extended Family Group," *American Sociological Review* 17 (1952), 297-306.

Bruce, Dickson D., Jr. *And They All Sang Hallelujah: Plain-Folk Camp-Meeting Religion, 1800-1845*. Knoxville: Univ. of Tennessee Press, 1974.

Campbell, John C. *The Southern Highlander and His Homeland*. 1921; rpt. Lexington: Univ. Press of Kentucky, 1969.

Caudill, Harry M. *My Land Is Dying*. New York: E. P. Dutton, 1973.

————. *Night Comes to the Cumberlands: A Biography of a Depressed Area*. Boston: Little, Brown, 1962.

Durkheim, Emile. *The Elementary Forms of the Religious Life*. Trans. Joseph Ward Swain. 1915; rpt. New York: Free Press, 1965.

Fisher, Stephen L. "Victim Blaming in Appalachia: Cultural Theories and the Southern Mountaineer." In *Appalachia: Social Context Past and Present*. Ed. Bruce Ergood and Bruce E. Kuhre. Dubuque, Iowa: Kendall/Hunt, 1976.

Ford, Thomas R. "The Passing of Provincialism." In *The Southern Appalachian Region: A Survey*. Ed. Thomas R. Ford. Lexington: Univ. of Kentucky Press, 1962.

————, ed. *The Southern Appalachian Region: A Survey*. Lexington: Univ. of Kentucky Press, 1962.

Frost, William G. "Our Contemporary Ancestors in the Southern Mountains," *Atlantic Monthly* 83 (March 1899), 311-19.

Geertz, Clifford. *The Interpretation of Cultures*. New York: Basic Books, 1973.

Geertz, Hildred, and Clifford Geertz. *Kinship in Bali*. Chicago: Univ. of Chicago Press, 1975.

Gennep, Arnold van. *The Rites of Passage*. Trans. Monika B. Vizedom and Gabrielle L. Caffee. Chicago: Univ. of Chicago Press, 1960.

Gerrard, Nathan L. "Churches of the Stationary Poor in Southern Appalachia." In *Change in Rural Appalachia: Implications for Action Programs*. Ed. John D. Photiadis and Harry K. Schwarzweller. Philadelphia: Univ. of Pennsylvania Press, 1970.

Goodenough, Ward H. *Description and Comparison in Cultural Anthropology*. Chicago: Aldine, 1970.

Hicks, George L. *Appalachian Valley*. New York: Holt, Rinehart and Winston, 1976.

Hooker, Elizabeth R. *Religion in the Highlands: Native Churches and Missionary Enterprises in the Southern Appalachian Area*. New York: Home Mission Council, 1933.

Kennedy, Gwen Neville. "Kinfolks and the Covenant: Ethnic Community Among Southern Presbyterians." In *The New Ethnicity: Perspectives from Ethnology*. Ed. John W. Bennett. Proceedings of the American Ethnological Society, 1973.

Kephart, Horace. *Our Southern Highlanders*. 1922; rpt. Knoxville: Univ. of Tennessee Press, 1976.

Knipe, Edward E., and Helen M. Lewis. "The Impact of Coal Mining on the Traditional Mountain Subculture." In *The Not So Solid South: Anthropological Studies in a Regional Subculture*. Ed. J. Kenneth Moreland. Southern Anthropological Society Proceedings, No. 4. Athens: Univ. of Georgia Press, 1971.

Leacock, Eleanor Burke, ed. *The Culture of Poverty: A Critique*. New York: Simon and Schuster, 1971.

Lewis, Helen M. "Fatalism or the Coal Industry?" *Mountain Life and Work* 46, No. 11 (Dec. 1970), 4–15.

Lewis, Oscar. "The Culture of Poverty," *Scientific American* 215 (1966), 19-25.

_____. *Five Families: Mexican Case Studies in the Culture of Poverty*. New York: Basic Books, 1959.

_____. *La Vida: A Puerto Rican Family in the Culture of Poverty—San Juan and New York*. New York: Random House, 1966.

MacClintock, S. S. "The Kentucky Mountains and Their

Feuds," *American Journal of Sociology* 7 (July, Sept. 1901), 1-28, 171-87.

Matthews, Elmora Messer. *Neighbor and Kin: Life in a Tennessee Ridge Community*. Nashville: Vanderbilt Univ. Press, 1966.

Pearsall, Marion. *Little Smoky Ridge: The Natural History of a Southern Appalachian Neighborhood*. University: Univ. of Alabama Press, 1959.

Photiadis, John D. "Rural Southern Appalachia and Mass Society." In *Change in Rural Appalachia: Implications for Action Programs*. Ed. John D. Photiadis and Harry K. Schwarzweller, Philadelphia: Univ. of Pennsylvania Press, 1970.

Photiadis, John D., and Harry K. Schwarzweller, eds. *Change in Rural Appalachia: Implications for Action Programs*. Philadelphia: Univ. of Pennsylvania Press, 1970.

Rosaldo, Renato. "Where Precision Lies: 'The hill people once lived on a hill.' " In *The Interpretation of Symbolism*. Ed. Roy Willis. ASA Studies 3. New York: John Wiley, 1975.

Schneider, David M. *American Kinship: A Cultural Account*. Englewood Cliffs, N.J.: Prentice-Hall, 1968.

———. "Kinship and Biology." In *Aspects of the Analysis of Family Structure*. Ed. Ainsley J. Coale et al. Princeton: Princeton Univ. Press, 1965.

———. "Kinship, Nationality, and Religion in American Culture: Toward a Definition of Kinship." In *Forms of Symbolic Action*. Ed. Robert F. Spencer. American Ethnological Society. Seattle: Univ. of Washington Press, 1969.

———. "Notes Toward a Theory of Culture." In *Meaning in Anthropology*. Ed. Keith H. Basso and Henry A. Selby. Albuquerque: Univ. of New Mexico Press, 1976.

———. "What is Kinship All About?" In *Kinship Studies in the Morgan Centennial Year*. Ed. Priscilla Reining. Washington, D.C.: Anthropological Society of Washington, 1972.

Schwarzweller, Harry K. "Social Change and the Individual in Rural Appalachia." In *Change in Rural Appalachia: Implications for Action Programs*. Ed. John D. Photiadis and

Harry K. Schwarzweller. Philadelphia: Univ. of Pennsylvania Press, 1970.

Semple, Ellen Churchill. "The Anglo-Saxons of the Kentucky Mountains: A Study in Anthropogeography," *Geographical Journal* 17 (June 1901), 588-623.

Shapiro, Henry D. *Appalachia on Our Mind: The Southern Mountains and Mountaineers in the American Consciousness, 1870-1920*. Chapel Hill: Univ. of North Carolina Press, 1978.

Stephenson, John B. *Shiloh: A Mountain Community*. Lexington: Univ. of Kentucky Press, 1968.

Toynbee, Arnold. *A Study of History*, Vol. II. 2nd ed.; London: Oxford Univ. Press, 1935.

Valentine, Charles A. *Culture and Poverty: Critique and Counter-Proposals*. Chicago: Univ. of Chicago Press, 1968. Review of Valentine, *Culture and Poverty. Current Anthropology* 10 (April-June 1969), 181-201.

Vance, Rupert B. "The Region: A New Survey." In *The Southern Appalachian Region: A Survey*. Ed. Thomas R. Ford. Lexington: Univ. of Kentucky Press, 1962.

Weller, Jack E. *Yesterday's People*. Lexington: Univ. of Kentucky Press, 1965.

Yanagisako, Sylvia Junko. "Introduction," Special Section: American Kinship, *American Ethnologist* 5 (Feb. 1978), 1-4.

INDEX

THE UNIVERSITY OF TENNESSEE PRESS
KNOXVILLE